The Scandal
of Christianity

---

the gospel
as stumbling block
to modern man

Emil Brunner

JOHN KNOX PRESS
ATLANTA

Fourth printing 1978

ISBN 0-8042-0708-9

LIBRARY OF CONGRESS CATALOG CARD NUMBER: 65-12729

© 1951 by W. L. Jenkins

Printed in the United States of America

Contents

I

Historical Revelation

In trying to formulate the purpose and topic of these lectures I have been wavering between choosing the plural or the singular of the word 'scandal'. Because each one of the five lectures deals with a specific aspect of the Christian message which might be called a scandal—in a sense which I shall justify and define presently—it might be said that there are many scandals. On the other hand, whilst the topic of each lecture is specific, they all have in common what is meant by the word 'scandal'.

To use this word of the Christian message sounds at first strange and even provocative. It is used here in its original New Testament sense. St. Paul, speaking in the first chapter of the first Epistle to the Corinthians of the centre of his whole gospel, says that it is a scandal, that is, a stumbling-block or offence, and foolishness to the unregenerate man. The message of Christ, notwithstanding the fact that it is the good news for all the world, is something against which the natural man cannot but react and revolt. Why is that so?

In the narrative of the synoptic gospels we read again and again that Jesus when approaching possessed persons met with the utmost resistance, as if he were an enemy

9

trying to enter a territory that is not his, and therefore has to be resisted. That territory, the human soul, is already occupied by an evil spirit claiming it as his property, on the legal basis, so to speak, of priority rights, and of having had undisputed dominion over it. According to New Testament teaching such possession by a dark power, which holds the soul of man in bondage, is not an exceptional condition found only in those who are called 'possessed'—though theirs may be a particularly grave and extreme form. But it is the condition of natural man as such, who by his sin, that is, by his separation from God his creator, has become a slave of the kingdom of darkness and rebellion against God.

Such a picture of natural man, of course, is most shocking to the average educated man of our age. It might be said, however, that the terrific happenings which the world has experienced during the last few decades, and similar ones which, unfortunately, seem to lie ahead of us as well, have made a good many of our contemporaries very sceptical of the typically modern view, that man is good, and more ready to acknowledge that there might be, after all, more truth in the New Testament teaching than in that of Rousseau and his followers. Since 1917 particularly, that is, since the era of totalitarian states began, the world has experienced such an outbreak of demonic forces that the complacent picture of optimistic evolutionism has been discredited as a true picture of man's nature, at least as far as the latest, specific manifestations of that nature are concerned.

If we look a little deeper, however, into the history leading up to this last phase of human history, we are bound to discover the fact that there is a more or less continuous spiritual development leading to and merging in it. The spiritual development of the western world, which we might indicate with such catchwords as secularism, naturalism and nihilism, was bound to end in these catastrophes and cataclysms. And again, behind this modern movement away from God and his law, there is fundamentally nothing else but what in the Bible is called sin.

We have to realize that in the New Testament the concept of sin is not, as in our modern use of the word, a merely moral one, but it embraces man's whole existence and his whole understanding of himself and the whole of life, let me say his philosophy, his ideologies and religion, as well as his personal life. Because his whole existence is perverted, under the control of negative powers, he is bound to resist the gospel of Christ. That is the reason why St. Paul speaks of the foolishness and the scandal of the message of Christ, and it is in this sense that he speaks.

Now this godless, hostile disposition of man with regard to the gospel has its specific form and expression in every age. It also has a different dynamic in different ages. This is true, particularly in the modern age, which for reasons that I cannot analyse now has been a specially fertile ground for the development of negative powers. The modern mind has its specific arguments against the gospel truth and therefore the scandal is also of a specific nature. The offence which the modern man takes at the gospel message is not exactly the same as in other times, although the basic nature of his opposition is the same as that of which the apostles and the Lord himself speak.

It is with reference to these specifically modern antitheses that I am going to try to develop some of the most important, and at the same time some of the most scandalous, doctrines of Christianity. They are *historical revelation* in this first lecture, *the triune God* in the second, *original sin* in the third, *the Mediator* in the fourth and *resurrection* in the fifth.

Among the educated people of our time there is a growing number who acknowledge the importance of religion for the spiritual and social life of humanity, and who themselves are not far from religious thinking and feeling. And amongst them there are many to whom in their personal life religion means something essential and indispensable. It is safe to say that the materialistic movement and even those of agnosticism and positivism have passed their climax. Among the intellectual leaders of our time we find more and more men who avow a religious faith. If, however, we ask what they mean by religion, their answers are not only very different, but also in most cases curiously indefinite. In one point only there is a general consensus of opinion—in the repudiation of all dogmatic religion. If we examine more precisely what is meant by this repudiation of the dogmatic, we discover that fundamentally it is the repudiation of a historical revelation. It is this which separates them from definite Christian faith. They refuse to be bound to something which happened once: they are out for religious immediacy. Certainly, they are looking for the divine, for the eternal, for a supra-historical meaning to all being and happening, they are searching passionately for the transcendently divine and trying to enter into relation with it, to be moved, to be filled, to be inspired and elevated by it. But they want this experience of the divine as something present and independent of anything belonging to the past. The intricate connexion in traditional Christian faith with past history, with a personality and certain happenings of far-away times, seems to them superfluous and embarrassing, unworthy and in any case uncertain. The eternal as something beyond time and therefore not in time; the divine as really divine and therefore not bound to a man; the experience of the divine here and now and therefore not mediated through some there and then: that is what they want. They agree with Fichte: 'It is not the historical but the metaphysical alone which saves.' Or with Lessing: 'Historical facts can never be a proof for eternal truth of reason.' And they all agree with Albert Schweitzer, who being an historian and knowing too well the unreliability and uncertainty of all historical tradition, seeks the foundation of religion in something beyond and independent of historical knowledge and historical doubt. Consequently, the form of religion towards which modern man inclines is mysticism, mystical religion being the religion of immediacy, of pure presence, free from historical connexions. Or it may be a religion similar to that which is found in Plato's doctrine of the eternal ideas, knowledge of a divine depth in his mystical awareness of eternal, timeless truth, knowledge hidden in his deepest self. Or, finally, it may be that rational theism which finds the Creator in the order of nature, and the moral Law-giver in the voice of conscience. Upholders of this kind of theism also speak of revelation, for they know that only a religion based on revelation can claim truth. But this revelation must be independent of history, it ought to be everywhere and at any time. This is the deep abyss which separates modern religion from Christian faith.

For what else can be the meaning of the word Christian but just this indispensable connexion with a historical event and person as the centre of this religion? Christian faith is faith in Jesus Christ as the supreme revelation of God. You cannot believe as a Christian without look-ing or pointing to this event of the past, without facing the divine revelation as having happened there and then. The question, then, which is put to us by modern men and which arises in each one of us, which therefore we cannot evade is, Why then this dependence on historical revelation? Why your Christian emphasis on an historical event? What do you Christians believe you have in your historical revelations, which we—in your opinion —do not have? Is it not just the other way round, that your connexion with history is a hindrance, a barrier, a minus not a plus, a sore embarrassment and not a gain? Why do you stick to that of all things?

The first answer to this question is very simple: because there and nowhere else we do find divine revelation.

The God in whom we believe is the one who can be found nowhere else but in Jesus Christ. If you ask why we believe in this revelation and this God and not in what you call revelation and God, we can simply answer, because this God has grasped us by this revelation and has by this truth and reality given us the conviction of his truth and reality. We believe as Christians have always believed, not because we have been taught so, but only because our faith comes from there alone, and is engendered from there again and again.

This is the first answer, but it is not the whole of our answer. We can and we should say what this historical element means to us, and this answer we shall try to give in what follows.

1. The historical event, that irrational givenness, is in exact correspondence with the irrational fact of our sin. Something has happened in us, we no longer live in the original innocence of divine creation, we have become— and this is the gloomy secret of our existence—sinners. Something is broken, a flaw, a breach has been made in the divine creation. We do not ask now, how, when, where this has happened (we may speak of it later on, for the moment it is immaterial). If it is true that sin does exist and that sin is guilt, then that flaw, that anomaly, that perversion of what ought to be is an undeniable irrational fact. What does that mean? Let us suppose that through some immediate revelation we know what God is—a supposition which, as we shall see later, is very doubtful, but which may be conceded for the argument's sake. For the moment, then, a second question has yet to be

answered, that question which means everything, namely, how this God, after the breach has been made, relates himself to us. This cannot be known by some immediate, timeless, eternal revelation. Such a timeless revelation, say by means of nature, can at best tell us who God is, the God who is the Creator, the God who wants us to live according to his law of creation. This revelation may tell us how he is related to us as long as we remain in his order of creation, but it can never tell us what his relation to us is after we have broken this order. Sin means that we have created a new situation, an historical and irrational situation, which cannot be deduced from any original order, but on the contrary is in contradiction to this original order. Therefore, that primeval knowledge which is related to the primeval situation does not give us any light. Conscience, for instance, can tell us what is God's request, what we ought to do, but it cannot tell us what is God's relation to those who have become disobedient to his commandment. It does not tell us how God, if I may use such human terms, reacts to the new situation which we have created.

2. There is a possibility of postulating God's reaction by deducing it from a given conception of God. Thus we might say that God is a kind Creator, therefore he will not let us perish, he will not let his creatures perish for having been disobedient to him; he cannot do that, because he is kind; he overlooks their guilt, he forgives 'as a matter of course'. This deduction, is, in substance, not different from that famous frivolity of the mocker Heine on his death-bed: 'Dieu pardonnera, c'est son

métier!' Anyone who has any grasp of the weight of the word sin and the words divine majesty and holiness, will know without a long proof that these words of Heine are the most brazen blasphemy which can be uttered. Whether God forgives or not, we cannot know by ourselves, by any timeless, immediate knowledge. Just as sin has happened, so forgiveness must happen, or else we remain in complete uncertainty as to what God's relation is to us, sinful rebels as we are.

3. As a matter of fact, the picture of that religion of immediacy, of which we were speaking, be it mystical, speculative or moralistic, corresponds exactly with our conclusion. It has no answer to the question of guilt. Forgiveness does not play a role in it. The question of guilt is simply ignored. That is to say, that irrational fact of the breach or flaw is ignored, just as a child that has lied to his mother thinks that his mother will not take it so seriously and will perhaps soon forget it. It is a striking conclusion, but after what we have said it is not surprising, but rather quite inevitable, that the question of guilt and forgiveness plays no role whatever in mystical, rationalist, moralist, idealist religion. The relation to God is established or thought of as established in a manner which shows no trace of that breach. Quite different things seem to be important—the expansion of the finite self to infinity, the knowledge of a divine original truth which has no relation to my personal being or personal situation, the experience of divine presence in which my being so or so, guilty or sinful, is of no concern. The religion of immediacy, therefore,

not troubling about historical revelation, does not trouble either about the historical element in my situation, that is, my sin and guilt. It treats it as non-existent.

Therefore this religion of immediacy is essentially and necessarily a religion of self-salvation. As this assertion seems to be in contradiction with at least some forms of religions, it is necessary to make certain qualifications. The most obvious form of the religion of self-salvation is to be found in that type of religion to which Kant in his book *Religion within the Limits of Pure Reason* has given classic expression. This is the more astounding as Kant in that very book has done something which hardly any philosopher of our epoch has done. He has acknowledged, on the basis of a very accurate and critical analysis of the concept and fact of moral evil, what he calls radical evil, which is a tendency to, or conspiracy with, unlawfulness which is found in every man, and which is inexplicable on the basis of the purely sensual or animal nature of man. This moral evil, he says, is a spiritual fact. It is a disobedience of the moral law whose origin he declares flatly to be not only unknown but unknowable. Therefore in order to get out of this moral evil not only a series of moral acts is necessary, but as he says, a revolution of disposition, a fundamental change of our moral condition. It is well known how Kant by this doctrine of radical evil aroused the strongest protests from almost all of his contemporaries. For instance, Goethe reproached him for this unpardonable compromise with the Christian doctrine of original sin and accused him of being a traitor, but evidently

18

without taking into account the fact that Kant himself was not inclined to draw the consequences of his own discovery. For who is, on Kant's view, the one who produces that moral revolution? None but man himself. There is in him something which does not seem to be touched by that radical evil. The innermost kernel, that moral autonomy of the will, by which man gives the moral law to himself, is intact, and from this basis of operation—if I may thus describe it—the revolution of the moral condition is possible. It is man himself who is capable of disentangling himself from evil and of replacing himself in the moral attitude which is pleasing to God. Self-salvation then is evident.

4. More important than this Kantian rationalistic form of religion is mysticism. I do not speak now of so-called Christian mysticism, but of that aboriginal mysticism, as we find it more or less identically in India, in Persia, in Greece and also in modern times. Mysticism in its logical structure is the same everywhere and in all times. Its programme is to find the way to knowledge or to emotional experience of complete unification with the divine being by plunging into the depth of the soul and by disentangling the soul from all impressions of the outward world. This is the *via mystica*, and it is a way taken by man himself, whatever the different stages of this way into the depth may be—it is man and always man alone who goes that way. Certainly God is thought of as somehow active, but this activity consists merely in a process similar to the air streaming into a room as soon as the window is opened; it is man who opens the

window, it is man who empties his soul by the *via mystica*, who therefore creates the conditions to make the divine come in. The initiative in this process is on man's side alone. This is the religion of self-salvation through mystical procedure.

5. An exception to this rule seems to be offered in the so-called grace mysticism of India, as we find it in the *bhakti* doctrine of Hinduism. We find here the word grace playing a large part, and indeed formulae which seem to offer exact parallels to the Augustinian, Lutheran doctrine of *sola gratia*. This doctrine seems to establish the total passivity of man and the sole activity of God in the extremest possible way in the so-called cat-rule as against the formula of the ape-rule. According to the ape-rule man behaves like a young monkey which clings by its own strength to its mother, which saves it from danger. According to the cat-rule, on the other hand, man's situation is that of a kitten which is taken in its mother's mouth and carried into safety by her act alone. We might therefore be led to interpret this, in terms of occidental tradition, as an extremely Augustinian or Lutheran conception of grace as against semi-pelagianism or synergism, which means a radical religion of grace without compromise, a radical refusal of self-salvation.

But if we look closer, we see that in reality what happens is not different from what happens everywhere in mysticism. Man gives himself through mystical meditation to the divine reality. Negatively speaking, the question of guilt and forgiveness is not raised here. The only concern is unification with the divine. No breach between God and man is seen, no new creation, no forgiveness of guilt. What is meant by grace, by the absolute passivity of man and the exclusive activity of God, is the expansion of the human self and its submersion in the divine. True, this unification is interpreted exclusively in terms of God's action and not man's. But the divine activity, divine grace, consists merely in making full what was empty, in giving man what he had not; there is no question of the gulf between man and God, nothing about forgiveness of sin. There is no salvation, no redemption from something which lies as an obstacle between God and man. The whole process means merely a supplementing, a perfecting of man's condition. If that is true of *bhakti*-religion, it is so much more true of modern mysticism, in which the experience of the infinite, boundless, timeless divine is the centre—as for instance in the nature mysticism of Whitman or the idealistic mysticism of Emerson. However different all these types of modern religions may be from one another, on one point they are agreed: guilt, the negative human situation caused by disobedience, and forgiveness of guilt, the new situation created by God's act of removing the obstacle and healing the breach, play no part in them.

6. This one thing then has become clear: religion of immediacy, which is not related to historical revelation and thinks this to be its privilege, ignores the central fact of human existence, that sin separates us from the holy God. If it is true that man is a sinner, if it is true that he is incapable of healing the breach which his sin has

opened between himself and the Creator, if it is true that he is involved in guilt from which he cannot free himself: if all this is true, then religion of immediacy is a falsification of the human situation and is possible only on the basis and in the power of this falsification.

This is made clear in the acknowledgement made by faith in historical revelation. When we as Christians say that only by an intervention of God, by his creating a new situation, can communion with God be established, we recognize that a breach between God and man does exist.

That is why historical revelation is the great scandal or stumbling-block for natural men. Man, filled with his self-love and self-pride, does not want to be uncovered, because he does not want his pride to be infringed upon. To acknowledge historical revelation means to acknowledge that the truth is not in us, that the right relation to God cannot be established from our side; that the breach between God and us is of such a nature that we can do nothing about it. On the other hand, religion of immediacy, be it of the mystical or the rationalistic or the idealistic type, means that the necessary presuppositions enabling us to establish the right relation to God, or to remove the obstacle between our present and the normal condition, lie in ourselves. Because it is the passionate interest of natural man, of natural self-love and self-pride, to keep this immediacy and to avoid the admission of his incapacity, he now proceeds to discredit historical revelation. Attacked by the gospel he follows the old strategic motto, that attack is the best defence, and

22

begins to attack. This attack he conducts on the following lines.

1. All historical revelation, like all historical traditions, can give only conditional and not unconditional certainty. Therefore religion cannot be, or ought not to be, tied to history. As directed against Christian faith this argument derives its strength from the fact of critical study of the Bible, which, it is asserted, has shaken the historical foundations of that faith. Nothing in the gospel stories, not to speak of the Old Testament, is free from doubt. Everything lies under the fire of critical examinations. Biblical criticism has turned the world of biblical, historical facts into a heap of ruins. Who would dare to erect an edifice of faith on such wreckage?

2. The second argument goes deeper. That which is historical is in itself relative; the absolute can never be, or become, historical. 'The idea,' says Strauss, 'does not care to pour all its fulness into a single individual and to be niggardly towards all the others.' Jesus Christ may have expressed divine truth in a high degree, in a particularly high degree, even in the highest degree, but he would not have exhausted it. Even he remains a man of history, and therefore a merely relative expression of the absolute. Inversely, the absolutization of an historical fact or an historical person is mythology. The thought that God became man, that in the years 1 to 30 once for all the salvation of the world has taken place, that Jesus Christ is not the *primus inter pares*, but the only one standing outside the series, that he is the God-man, the Mediator, all that is mythology, mythology transformed

23

by false personification, by absolutizing an historical event, making an eternal truth into a divine history. 'God-history' is myth. A God who becomes man, a God-man who is Word become flesh, all that is mythology, unbearable to thinking man, though for the primitive mind it may be an adequate form of comprehension of ideal truth. The idea of a divine being becoming man cannot be reconciled with the idea of the changeless eternity of the Godhead: it is an assault against the sublimity of the idea of God.

3. The third argument is that belief in an historical revelation makes faith irrational and makes the faithful intolerant. What kind of a God is he, who one day in the year 1 or 30 does or gives what mankind should have had long ago for its salvation? This arbitrariness of histor- ical revelation, which gives at a certain point in history a divine light into the dark world, but leaves the world before that event and the world outside of it in the dark, is unbearable to our sense of divine justice. On the other hand, the assertion that Christians alone possess the full divine truth must make them arrogant and intolerant towards the others, who are not able to do anything about it: they are simply not the privileged ones, and their religion must be devaluated as superstition and mere paganism.

These are, so far as I can see, the main arguments which since the time of Celsus have been raised against Christian faith, against its centre. What is our answer?

1. To the first point we answer: Certainly, historical traditions are of merely relative certainty, they are open

to historical criticism, even to historical scepticism. That is true, as we know, of the gospel stories, and must be acknowledged. Historical criticism has transformed the gospels into a field of ruins and all attempts to restore a gospel harmony and all protests of fundamentalism are vain. It is a curious thing, however, that the recognition of this fact has not been able to shake the Christian faith of some of the most critical of historians. The Jesus who encounters us in these fragmentary and precarious traditions, is for them, is for us, as he always was, Christ, the Son of God, the God-man, and the uncertainty of historical knowledge as such does not alter the fact that faith in him carries with it absolute certainty. If we ask how this is possible, the answer must be that God, even through these historically precarious testimonies, can bring before us his Son as the incarnate Word, and testify to him through his Spirit, so as to fill us with absolute certainty. The certainty of faith lies on another plane than the secular certainty of historical facts. Whilst the Gospel traditions, considered as historical documents by the historian, carry with them not more than relative certainty, they become to the believer through the divine Spirit the instrument of the Word of God, which in itself has absolute certainty, as—to use a worldly image— the flawless beauty of a symphony of Mozart may reach us even through the very precarious medium of a gramophone-record.

2. To the second point we answer: The question of myth divides the spirits. Here is where the decision takes place. For rational thought, not only God's becoming

man, but any thought of a God who takes an initiative in the world, is mythology. The argument of myth extends as far as the idea of the personal living God as such. If God is an idea, then this argument holds. An idea can never be completely expressed in the finite, and all expressions of the idea are merely relatively different from each other. But if God is not an idea, if he is a living God, as the whole Bible testifies that he is, then his intervention in history, his coming to men, the Son of God becoming man, is no mythology, but the manifestation of that divine self-movement, that divine livingness which is the essence of his being. So much can be said: the belief in historical revelation engenders also another conception of God which differs from those held by all mysticism, rationalism or idealist speculation. Of that the next lecture will say more. But the idea not only of God but also of the meaning and goal of man's existence is different in the two cases. In the first, where God is thought of as a timeless idea, the ultimate aim is unity, whilst in biblical faith the aim is community. In the first case the meaning of life is knowledge, in the second the meaning is love. From the point of view of the rational idea of God, the Christian faith is false, but also from the point of view of the Christian faith the rational idea of God is false. Neither can be proved. The decision is the decision of faith. That is to say, whether we believe in one or the other is dependent on whether historical revelation makes us respond or whether we dodge it. Holding fast the rational idea of God, you can escape humiliation and dependence and you can hold fast as long as you want to escape. But the moment you no longer escape but accept the humiliation, that rational idea, and with it the whole argument of mythology, breaks down. The decision, then, is no other than whether or not you accept or refuse the appellation of a sinner.

3. To the third point, why God has elected Israel out of all people as his people, why the Son of God has become man in the years 1 to 30 in Palestine and not long before in China or India, and in all times and at once, we can add, why has God made this world and not another one? why has he made large and small beasts, large and small stars? Why has he created innumerable non-rational creatures and only so few rational ones? To all these questions we shall have no answer in this life, but they cannot be seriously put by anyone who bends himself before the majesty and omnipotence of God the Creator. We do not live together with God in a democracy of heaven and earth. In a democracy any citizen can at any time require an account from the government of what it does. We are not living, however, in a democracy in this world, but in an absolute monarchy, and between God and ourselves there is no other equality but that which was his free gift, which he bestows on us as his image. Democracy is a good thing to order human relations, but the idea of equality which is basic to it cannot be applied to the relation between God and man, so as to call to account God the Creator as one calls to account the president or the prime minister. The end of true reverence is the end of true religion.

So far as the reproach of intolerance and arrogance is concerned, there is a misunderstanding. He who has been given grace as a sinful man and now wants to share this grace with his fellow-man—that grace which he receives undeservedly—cannot be intolerant or arrogant. He will be tolerant and humble as long as he does not forget that the truth which he has is not his but God's, and that it is meant not for him only, but for all mankind. It is true, unfortunately, that very often Christians *have* had that false intolerant and arrogant attitude towards non-Christians; but the true missionary spirit surging from Christ's love to mankind is the very opposite of arrogance and intolerance. In fact, we may say, love as grounded in Jesus Christ is the only sure antidote against arrogance and intolerance, because this love springs from the humiliation of man, who acknowledges that truth is not in him, but comes to him, has come to him, and must come to him always, if he is to stay in it. And that truth can never be his own property, but is always a present of divine mercy.

Therefore the question whether we need historical revelation or not, is a question which is decided by faith alone; a question, then, which is not decided by intellectual pros and cons, but only in that ultimate decision which claims the totality of man, namely, whether our honour and justification lie in ourselves, or whether we have to receive them from outside ourselves. We know how Christian faith decides. We know now why faith has to decide so. And this must be the last word in this matter.

II

The Triune God

THERE was never a time in history when man did not worship something divine. The idea that there is a supra-human reality seems to spring up with a certain necessity in the mind of man, and is not lacking even where it is rejected as a mere fancy or as characteristic of a low phase in the evolution of human knowledge. We find the idea of God in two realms of spiritual life, first and fore-most in that of religions, that is, in forms of worship which are a part of the life of nations and even larger units, imposing upon their life a certain uniform struc-ture. Secondly we find it in the realm of individual philosophical thought, as a part of the metaphysical systems of individual eminent thinkers, who in con-nexion with their enquiries into the ultimate principles of being have been obliged to acknowledge the idea of a divine being or of the divine character of being as an inevitable, necessary and integral part of their system.

In the realm of religions the idea of God shows an almost unlimited variety. This variety can be to a certain extent classified. It seems, however, impossible to find a common denominator, since there are irreconcilable contradictions within the variety. First, the opposition of the personal and the impersonal. Primitive religion at the lowest stage of its evolution is impersonal. The divine reality that Otto calls the numinous has more the character of an 'it' than of a he or she. It is like an atmospheric power which cannot be grasped or a kind of fluid which imparts itself to certain things or manifests itself in certain phenomena. Polytheism is on a higher stage of evolution. But within the different pantheons we find gods of the most different characters, different in their disposition and their manner of acting as well as in the rank which they hold. There are dark and light, evil and good, low and high gods; there are hierarchies with a more or less monarchical apex and with a whole gamut of beings of superhuman power, with half-gods or heroes at the lower end of the divine scale who form a transition to earthly men. Leaving this polytheistic mythology and coming to the so-called higher religions, we find in them similar contradictions or opposites. We see there, in one of the highest, most spiritual religions, the dualistic opposition of the good and the evil god ; or we see some of them highly personal and some highly impersonal in their conception of the divine principle. We even have, in original Buddhism, the strange phenomenon of a religion without God. In all these instances, the attempt to combine these ideas even in the most modest way with the Christian idea must lead to failure.

The case is different with the two clearly monotheistic religions, with Judaism and Islam. Here a certain kinship and similarity with Christianity cannot be denied. Common historical roots may partly account for this fact. It would hardly be possible to justify the assertion that the Lord of Judaism and the Allah of Islam have no positive relation to the Christian idea of God. All the same, every missionary in the Jewish or Mohammedan mission-field knows well enough that here the opposition becomes particularly acute. It is the doctrine of the triune God which is at once the centre of Christian thought about God and the cause of the most acute and most passionate rejection by these two monotheistic religions. It is this doctrine of the Trinity which also separates the Christian from all philosophical, speculative, rationalist ideas of God.

As we have just stated, it is not religion alone which produces the idea of God. Since the metaphysical doctrine of Greek philosophers, there has always been in the west a tradition of philosophical theology, which in the course of western history has developed alongside the Christian conception of God, as it is grounded in biblical revelation. These two streams have mutually affected one another in very different ways. Sometimes they have merged into one another, sometimes the one has been dominated by the other, sometimes—and this has been particularly true in modern times—the philosophical idea of God has almost discarded the Christian one, not only within the limited circle of the philosophically minded, but also in the large masses of western humanity. It may be that the contours of this popularized philosophical idea of God have become very vague; none the less its origin in philosophy, and thus its difference from the Christian conception, is unmistakable.

31

What we said about the enormous variety of religious ideas of God is true also of the philosophical. There is not one, but there is a great variety of philosophical ideas of God. The God of pantheism is different from that of deism or that of theism. The God of Plato is not the same as the God of Heraclitus, or that of Aristotle or of Neoplatonism. The God of Spinoza is different from that of Leibnitz, of Kant, of Fichte, of Hegel. Into our own time the multiplication of ideas of God has not ceased—I mention only the philosophical theology of William James and that of Josiah Royce. It is to be noted that as the Greek philosophical ideas of God influenced the Christian doctrine, so these different philosophical theologies of the post-Christian era in their turn were influenced more or less by the conception of God in the Christian biblical tradition.

It may therefore seem a very bold undertaking to consider these different philosophical ideas of God as a unity and to confront them with the Christian conception. All the same, this is possible along the same line of demarcation as appeared between Christianity and the two monotheistic religions, in the same sense and for the same reason: the God of the philosophers is not the triune God of Christian faith. For the sake of simplicity, I shall confine myself, in what follows, explicitly to the philosophical conceptions of God, for the moment not dealing with the religious ones. We shall come back to this side of the problem later on.

If we say that the Christian idea of God is that of the triune God, this means first that the God of our faith is the one who revealed himself in Jesus Christ. The Christian doctrine of the Trinity has its fundamental importance for Christian theology primarily in this, that it points towards the necessary connexion between revelation and the idea of God—to be more exact, to the relation between the biblical conception of God and the revelation in Jesus Christ. The Bible expresses this in the simplest and most understandable way by saying that God is the Father of our Lord Jesus Christ. This is to say, the God whom we know through his revelation in Jesus Christ is not the same God as the one we think we know outside this revelation. The manner by which we know God implies then another content of our knowledge. This becomes particularly clear if we compare the idea of God in philosophical, metaphysical theology with that of the Christian doctrine.

Whatever the content of the philosophical ideas of God may be in detail one trait of character is common to all: it is a man-thought God, a God who is found by way of thinking, or negatively it is not a God who reveals himself in history. This is the distinction in that saying of Pascal's which is a part of the famous document which was found at his death sewed into his vest, and which has been called his spiritual testament, 'Dieu d'Abraham d'Isaac et de Jacob non des philosophes', the God of philosophy is not the same as the God of biblical revelation. Even if we knew nothing else of the philosophical idea of God than this one thing, that it is reached or acquired by philosophical thinking, we would know by that the most essential thing, namely that this God is not a God of revelation. The God of philosophers is an idea of their thinking, a content posited on the ground of certain philosophical reflections, as a more or less integral part of their philosophical system. So Plato's idea of God forms the crown of his doctrine of ideas. So Aristotle's idea of God is the apex of his doctrine of the entelechies. So the Neoplatonic idea of God is the terminal point of that speculation which proceeds by way of abstraction from the concrete data of sensual experience to that all-comprehensive abstraction, the idea of being or the one and all. So Spinoza's idea of God is identical with the fundamental conception of his metaphysics, the concept of substance which, unknowable in itself, manifests itself in the two attributes, in spatial being and in thought or conceptual being, and which for that reason can as well be named God or nature. Or again, in the newer systems of philosophical theism, God is the necessary presupposition for the being as such and the particular nature of the empirical world.

It is not our intention to deny any justification, or even necessity, to such metaphysical theologies. We leave it to the philosophers to decide the legitimacy of this procedure and its results. We should not lose sight of the fact, however, that there is a plurality of such systems and their corresponding ideas of God, each of which claims for itself the same necessity and strictness of argument which those who deny the legitimacy of philosophical theology also claim. So that, up to this moment as throughout the last 2500 years, the mutual rivalries and denunciations of the different systems have made it difficult for anyone to give the full credit of philosophical proof to any one of them. What we now emphasize and wish to demonstrate is one thing only, that the philosophical idea of God is necessarily different from that of faith based on revelation. Even if all philosophers reached one and the same theological result, and even if this result were unambiguously a theistic idea of God, we should still have to maintain what we have maintained, that the God of philosophy is a different God from the God of revelation. He is not a God who manifests himself as speaking and acting, by his own initiative, in historical revelation. The God of philosophy is, by definition, an idea acquired by man's own thinking. This does not mean to say that the idea does not claim objective reality. All philosophers would endeavour to show that their idea of God, which imposes itself by necessity, has objective reality. But it is also clear that this God is not a living God in the sense of the biblical testimony, that is, in the sense of a personal reality intervening in the course of human history. It is not a Thou addressing man: 'I am the Lord Thy God.' It is the movement of man's own thought, which, so to say, in its end reaches God. The initiative, the movement leading towards knowledge, lies entirely on the side of the human mind, not on the side of God. It is a God whom to reach lies within the possibilities of human thinking. It is not a God who, from outside human capacities, enters by his own movement and by his own initiative into the thought-world of men and, so to say, bursts open the closed globe of human thought. Such a God is the one who says: 'I am the Lord Thy God.' The philosophical doctrine which always to a certain extent—and now more than ever—opposes the Christian doctrine, claims as its distinctive mark of truth that it does not imply such mythological or anthropocentric conceptions as that of a self-speaking, self-moving God. From its point of view, this conception of a God breaking into human experience and thoughts from outside is nothing but a primitive anthropomorphism which is below the dignity of mature thinking.

On the other hand, it is this very fact of divine self-manifestation, breaking open the immanent structure of human thought and opening to man an otherwise closed transcendent reality, to which faith clings. If in faith we speak of God, we mean this very God who reveals himself, self-operating, self-affirming, self-disclosing, unknown and unreachable by any kind of human mental exertion outside his own act of self-revelation. That this revelation is a reality, that it is really God who speaks and not a voice of man's own psyche or spirit, falsely interpreted as a revelation—this of course cannot be proved. Why not? Because proving is exactly, by definition, what human thought handles in its own capacity and competence. What is capable of proof is by definition immanent in thought, just as revelation by definition transcends thought and is therefore incapable of proof. Faith as it understands itself is a real encounter in which something happens that cannot happen within man's own thought-life. But while the reality of this happening cannot be proved, but only experienced—in that

36

experience which we call faith—something else can be and ought to be proved, namely the difference between the conception of God which comes about in this way, and that which is produced within philosophical thinking. This different content of the conception of God is given in the testimony of the Bible and it is of this content in its distinction from all other ideas of God that we shall now speak.

1. The first difference, which is at the same time the fundamental characteristic of the Christian concept of God, is that God is understood as the Lord. This implies the unconditional sovereignty and freedom of God. God is under no necessity whatever, apart from that which he himself establishes. God is the Creator of the universe. Where God is an idea of philosophy and not faith's experience of revelation, you will always find a relationship of necessity between God and the universe. Even where he is called the Creator, the idea that God can be what he is without a universe, is hardly possible within a philosophical doctrine of God; at any rate, I do not know of any great philosophical theologian who has put forward such an idea. On the contrary, even the theists establish between God and creature what is called a correlative relation, that is a relation of such a kind that as the world cannot be without God, God cannot be without the world. Otherwise how could philosophical thought reach the idea of God, starting from the knowledge of the world? The biblical doctrine of God takes the freedom of God absolutely seriously. In freedom, and that means out of nothing, God creates

the world as he pleases. And this world stands in every moment solely in the power of this divine act. Although this idea of unconditional sovereignty is a fundamental element of all biblical doctrine about God, it is only in the trinitarian conception that its ultimate consequence is grasped. That God alone who in himself is loving and therefore needs no creatures in order to be the loving God—and this is what is meant by the doctrine of the Trinity—is in his own being entirely independent of the being of the world and therefore perfectly sovereign. The existence of the world in no way completes the character of God.

2. With this first element a second is intimately bound up. The world, although it exists only through divine acts, is a real opposite, a reality over against God. This reality of the creature is, at its maximum, human freedom. It is so real that man in his creaturely freedom can in reality contradict God's will. God has, if I may say so, taken the risk of creating such a creature, which, although it is by no means divine, is given the power to contradict the Creator. In this idea of creation the distinction between God's being and created being is clear-cut. God alone is God, to him alone belongs the attribute of the divine, and the creature is nothing but the creature and therefore in no way divine. The concept of cosmos, common to all antiquity, namely the idea of a divine universe and a divinity immanent in the universe, is dissolved.

3. It is this monopoly of divinity which is the central element of the biblical doctrine of God, namely his

holiness. God and the world must never be confused, but kept in sharpest distinction. In God there is nothing of creatureliness and in the world there is nothing of divinity. The being of God and the being of creatures are totally different. On the one hand there is the transcendent Godhead and on the other the radical creatureliness of the world. This distinction of being or nature must, however, not be confused with the negation of God's immanence or activity in this world which he has created.

By the holiness of God we understand not merely this difference of being but also that God wants to be acknowledged in his absolute sovereignty and wants to make manifest his lordship over the world. Man, the highest of his creatures, is destined to acknowledge this lordship and to honour him. The Lord God wants to make his lordship over the creature a reality. This is the character of the God of the Bible, this Lord Jahwe who does not want to share his glory with anyone else, but keep it to himself alone. Only so can we understand what the Bible calls the kingdom of God. In this idea the two elements are contained: (1) that God wants to be Lord, that all creatures shall be full of his glory, and (2) that the creature, man, has a relative God-given independence and is expected to give God by trust and obedience what he requires. It is from this point that the ethical character of faith originates as the foundation of all Christian ethics. The will of God, his reign, is such that it can be realized only by free obedience. God leaves room for the free act of his creature. The realism of his lordship is not a perfect thing at the outset, but an ethical or moral task, something which is not in the beginning but is the end of history.

Having reached this point, let us glance at the philosophical idea of God, whether it be that of Plato or Aristotle, of Neoplatonism or of Spinoza. Nowhere in these systems does the question arise of this will of God to reign. Neither the idea of ideas, nor the one and all, nor the first mover, nor the absolute substance is a Lord God who wants to have his will acknowledged by his creature. The impersonal character of all these ideas leaves no room for such a moral historical dynamism. That is true also of what is known as philosophical theism. It is true that the moral law, as the expression of the divine will, plays an important part in this system, but the divine law as formulated there does not contain this idea of God's honour or glory. It does not express this will to reign, this energy of self-expression in the sanctification of all creatures. On the contrary, in all times this biblical thought, that God wants to have his honour acknowledged, has given rise to criticism and even scorn on the part of the philosophers. They look on it as the expression of a mythological anthropocentricism, a rather low conception of the supreme reality. The God of the philosophers is not the holy God, who wills himself absolutely and who reacts with divine wrath against those who resist him. God's honour or glory and God's wrath have no place within a philosophical concept of God. Why not? Because the God of the philosophers is not the God of revelation, but of thought. He is not a

God who stands over against man as the Lord-creator, but he is a principle which man finds necessary in order to explain reality. From the point of view of philosophical theology this biblical Lord God, like the self-speaking, self-acting personal God, is, as we have already pointed out, mythology. If rational thought is the ultimate judge in theology, this biblical personalism in the idea of God, as in the idea of revelation, is bound to be rejected.

Here a remark on 'person' may be useful. What is personality as distinguished from anything else? A person is a being of such a kind that we cannot ourselves think it, but it reveals itself to us in an act of revelation. What I myself think is the object of my thought. Even when I think God as a personal being this God is the object of my thought and therefore not truly personal. He can be something different from an object of thought only if it is not myself who think him, but himself who reveals himself by an act of self-disclosure. Everything which I think myself, or the reality which is disclosed by my own mental activity, is therefore not a person. A person is that unique being which discloses itself and therefore enters into my thought-world, so to say, as a stranger, affirming itself as an I in its own right. In my own thought-world I am the unchallenged centre, I am the subject of all objects of my thought, and by that, so to say, the master of them all. When, however, a person encounters me, a rival world-centre faces me, a kind of being which refuses to be a part of my thought system. This is the absolutely unique fact of meeting a Thou. God as personal God is the God who does not allow himself to be placed amongst the objects of my thought, but claims not only to be a self, like myself, but the real centre of all I's and I-worlds. And this is exactly what is meant by the Lord God revealing himself as Lord. Perhaps this becomes clearer when we come to consider the second fundamental trait of the revealed essence of God, namely divine love and mercy.

We have already pointed out, in our first lecture, that the question of historical revelation corresponds to the fact that there has been a breach in our relationship with God. How should the man who has broken the original relation with God know how the holy God, the Lawgiver and Lord, will react to this transgression? The law is by definition something unchangeable, static, something which endures in timeless eternity, the eternal will of God. Out of the law therefore you can never know what will be God's attitude towards such creatures as have broken the law. From the point of view of the law there would be one possibility only, the destruction of this rebellious creature, the impossibility, that is, that he should continue to exist. If a man in moral earnestness were to draw this consequence, he would stumble over the fact that he still exists and therefore would begin to doubt whether God takes his own law seriously. The divine law therefore leaves him in uncertainty about the actual relation of God towards him. Therefore it is the revelation of forgiving, redeeming grace which more than any other makes clear what a miracle revelation is. One thing is certain: forgiving grace, justification of the sinner, pardoning the rebel, receiving into communion the one who has merited divine wrath—all this cannot be known by any rational process—and that is what philosophical theology indirectly confirms; it never speaks of this grace. This is exclusively the content of historical revelation, beginning with the Old Testament, reaching its summit in the message of that unconditional forgiveness which we find in the doctrine of justification of the sinner through Jesus Christ. Here alone, in the New Testament testimony to Christ, do we find that word which may be called the heart of the Christian conception of God: God is love. You cannot imagine this word being found in a book of Plato or Kant. Forgiveness of sin is the expression of the incomprehensible renewal of God's relation to us, known or knowable only through an incomprehensible act of divine revelation.

From the point of view of philosophy such an assertion is completely irrational, and forgiveness of sin complete nonsense. The philosopher—I am speaking always of the philosopher who takes no account of divine revelation in Christ—being obliged to give reasons for what he says, can only acknowledge a reasonable God, that is, a God who acts logically. If God is the lawgiver, then he must cling to his law and by some means or other remove resistance to it; or if God desires unconditionally the life and the well-being of his creatures, then he must ignore the evil. Each of these two attitudes can be called rational or logical. But to assert at one and the same time the holiness of God's will, reacting against transgression, his wrath, *and* his merciful forgiveness of guilt, is a paradox which rational philosophy can only decline as absurdity. This is what the New Testament itself says, the message of the cross is foolishness to the Greek.

The message of the cross is the unity of these two, the holiness of God demanding the destruction of the transgressor and the love of God saving the sinner. The message of the cross says first, that the wrath of God is a reality inseparable from the fact of sin. The holy God cannot ignore the creature's resistance to his will. He would, so to say, abandon himself, deny his holiness in merely ignoring human rebellion. The divine wrath must manifest itself as a deadly reaction of the Holy against the unholy. But it says, secondly, that God does not want the death of the sinner but his salvation. God's love is greater than man's sin, he forgives guilt however great it may be. This paradoxical unity of holiness and mercy, which is inaccessible to rational thought, is the message of the Bible.

Having reached this point, let us pass in review for a moment the religious history of mankind on its heights. We ask the question: Is there to be found anywhere outside the Bible, outside biblical revelation, this unity of holiness and forgiving mercy? There are religions, as for instance Parseeism, in which there is something known of the holy will of God, of his lordship over the universe, and of the moral aim of history. If we ignore for the moment the dualism of the religion of Zarathustra and consider only its teaching that finally the good God becomes Lord and manifests his superiority in his victory, there seems to be here a real parallel to the prophetic religion of Israel, and it is significant enough that this religion has issued from a prophetic personality, the man Zarathustra. But if we look closer, this parallel does not hold. The religion of Zarathustra knows nothing of forgiveness of sin, of divine mercy. The holiness of God simply destroys the evil and remunerates the good. They, the good ones, share the victory of the good principle. In that last judgment where all men have to pass over the abyss upon a cobweb, the good ones pass, the bad ones are dashed hopelessly into the abyss of perdition. This religion knows nothing of the fact that we are all sinners and have all merited death. Therefore there is no need for the thought and the proclamation of forgiveness, of saving grace.

The same is true, in principle, of Islam. The idea of divine forgiveness is not entirely foreign to it, but taking the Koran as a whole, the idea of forgiveness does not have any decisive place within that system of rigid legal moralism. Allah is a good and holy God, but he is not that holy one who is at the same time the Merciful Father. Jesus' word that God is love is unthinkable here. Islam, like Parseeism, is a religion of moral legalism with a moralistic eschatology, in which nothing matters but the norm of obedience to the law.

Finally, Judaism. Judaism, like Christianity, acknowledges as its source the Old Testament revelation. This is the common root out of which the close relationship which is apparent at the very first glance is to be explained. Where then do the two depart from one another? Why is it that the Jews have to this very day not been able to acknowledge in Jesus Christ the Messiah whom they expect? Because Jesus is the crucified. It is true that the Jews accept the prophetic message not only of a holy but also of a merciful God. This paradox is not unknown to them, for their doctrine of God too, like that of Christianity, is not philosophical, but is based on historical revelation. The Jews also know of forgiveness of sin and acknowledge that even the most righteous need it. But the radical conception of sin which is embodied in the New Testament and therefore radical forgiveness as expressed in the justification of the sinner through the reconciling suffering and death of the Saviour seems to them to be unbearable, even blasphemous. As the cross of Christ is foolishness to the Greek, that is to the philosophical mind, it is a scandal or stumbling-block to the Jews. In the last analysis, as Paul has shown again and again, they cannot accept the radical message of free grace.

The unity of holiness and mercy in God is exclusively the Christian idea of God, and this conception is strictly related to the historical revelation of the life ending with the death on the cross of Golgotha. This is the answer which has been given to the human question, What is the attitude of the holy God to sinful men? The answer of the New Testament is that radical holiness, implying divine wrath against sin, and radical grace freely bestowing divine sonship upon the sinner, are put together in the way, inaccessible to any rational explanation, which is given in the supreme act of revelation.

We have so far seen two essential characteristics of the Christian idea of God, first that God is the one who reveals himself in history as the living Lord, who cannot be found by man's own thinking but who, being the absolute Subject which never can become man's object, can be known only by his self-disclosure; second that he reveals himself as the holy one who claims everything for himself and as that love which gives itself in free grace. We have now to proceed one more step and by doing so we find the unity of these two characteristics. We shall see that this last step leads us to the very core of the Christian message as it is formulated in the doctrine of the God-manhood of Christ and of the triune God.

Revelation means God's self-disclosure. It is not revelation about something. As long as it is that, as long as it is a word about God—even a prophetic word about God—it is not full revelation. God being Subject, person, cannot perfectly reveal himself except in personal presence. Immanuel, God himself present with us, dwelling amongst us, speaking to us, in the unity of revealing person and revealed person, so that the speaker is the same as the one of whom he speaks: that is what the New Testament gospel preaches. In Jesus Christ we encounter the holy and merciful God *in persona*. The one who is faced by Jesus Christ is faced by the absolute authority, claiming man for himself in the totality of his being. The one who is faced by Jesus Christ is faced by the loving God, giving himself for man. At the same time he is faced by a Man who perfectly obeys the holy will of God in perfectly giving himself as the instrument of God's saving grace. That Man, Jesus, is the only one who does do what all men ought to do: he lives in perfect love. In doing this and being this he reveals both the mystery of God's being and the mystery of man's being. He reveals God's being as holy love; he reveals man's reality as a sinner, for whose redemption God gives himself; and he reveals man's true being, namely living in God's own love.

Just as little as we know what and who God is, before he reveals his reality to us in personal presence, just as little do we know who man is, both in his untrue reality as a sinner and in his God-destined truth, before we see our sin and receive our true being in Jesus Christ. Jesus Christ is at the same time the revelation of true divinity and of true humanity, of God's sovereign loving personality and of man's personality as dependent on God's love. Nor do we know, apart from Christ (because we do not know what love is), either that love which is God's essence, free spontaneous love, or that love which makes up the true human being, namely living in God's love and in complete dependence on his giving. It is by the same act that God and man are revealed to us, in the God-man. This is one of the two great mysteries, that of Incarnation or the God-man.

The other, that of the Trinity, is included in it on the one hand, and is its foundation on the other hand. We have to distinguish, however, between the biblical and the later church doctrine of the Trinity. The Bible student, approaching the Scriptures from the side of church doctrine, cannot fail to see that the New Testament has no explicit doctrine of the Trinity. In some way one might even say the New Testament is not interested in the Trinity. It is, however, not only interested but it has its centre of gravity in the statement of the identity of the revealer Jesus Christ with the revealed God. That the love of Christ is really God's love and not merely human love—that is the one and all of the Gospel. It is here, in Christ, that we are faced with God's love and nowhere else; and it is God's love, it is God's own secret which is opened to us, God's own Life and Being which take hold of us in Christ. This one thing, in its two aspects, is what the New Testament stands for.

Now, that means that Jesus, so far as he is the giver and revealer of God's love—apart from whom this love is neither known nor given—is one with the source of this love. As the given love he is different from God, as the love-giver he is identical with him. As revelation, he is different from the revealed God; as revealer, he is identical with him. But in both respects, as the giver and as the given, he stands opposite us, opposite all humanity, as bringing into it that which it does not have and does not know and cannot know apart from him. And these two, inseparable from each other, this unity and this distinction, is what is meant by the Trinity of God, the Holy Spirit being the one by whom the objective, historical revelation becomes a revelation to us, subjectively. It is by the Holy Spirit that God makes us see the unity which is between himself and the revealer Jesus Christ.

That is the extent of the interest of the New Testament in the Trinity. But the question, how the three can be one and what are the relations between these three, lies outside the biblical interest. Perhaps theology has to enter into these questions, but certainly not because they are the real thing to be known by faith, but merely in order that the chief thing might not be misunderstood. That God was in Christ, essentially, in personal presence, and that what we have in Christ is really God, and that we have him through the Holy Spirit, who, again, is the same God—that is what we have to know. It is the mystery of God's true revelation and of the identity of God's nature with Christ's nature—but not the mystery of the Trinity—which we have to adore and to praise. We have not to see the three Persons alongside each other on the divine throne, but we have to see the love of the Father revealed and given through the Son by the Holy Spirit, so to say one behind the other in the order of their relation to us. We have the Father, through the Son, by the Holy Spirit.

Now we understand why no philosophy can reach the true God: because the true God is the one giving himself in love and thereby revealing himself as love. And now we can also see that this revelation is different from all that has been claimed to be revelation in the world of religions. Now we see why just those religions of which we might think they are closest to the biblical gospel are its most violent opponents. It is the scandal of God's holy love, giving itself to sinful men in the person of the crucified Lord, against which natural man even in his highest religious aspirations reacts, because and so long as he wants to defend himself against the humiliation of not being able to find God and please God himself, but has to be found by God, in his free grace.

III

Original Sin

THE question, who is God, is one question; the question, who is man, is another. Between these two questions there does not seem to be a necessary relation. Today there are not so many who ask about God because this question either does not interest them or they consider it unanswerable. No thinking man, however, can dodge the question, who he is himself, and this question seems to lie within the reach of human experience and knowledge. How should we not know who we are ourselves, since we are the nearest object of our knowledge—the object of our knowledge of which we have the richest and most intimate experience? All the same, the history of the efforts of man in this field show that it does not seem to be so easy to know oneself. It was not for nothing that *gnothi seauton* was the inscription on the temple of Delphi, where it was not the things of everyday knowledge but the hidden things which were proclaimed. It cannot be by chance that one of the greatest philosophers, Socrates, made the study of man, or the self-knowledge of man, the centre around which all his philosophical enquiries turned.

If we review the history of human knowledge from

the most ancient times to the most recent, we observe a curious fact, the similarity between the most primitive and the most recent idea of man. The oldest, most primitive stage of human thought about man shows us that man first placed himself entirely within his surrounding nature, not drawing a sharp line of demarcation between himself and the other animals. He seems to have looked on himself as a kind of animal and on the other hand to have looked on the animal as a kind of man, each similar to the other. And this most primitive view is also the most modern view. Since the renewal of biological science, as it is particularly characterized by the name of Darwin, men have begun again to consider themselves as a part of nature and man as a genus within the class of mammals. The methods of acquiring knowledge have changed since the time of primitive man, but the result is very similar. Perhaps the return of modern man to primitive, and by that I mean collectivist forms of life, as seems to be the trend of evolution, is the explanation of this similarity. For so much can be stated in advance, that what man thinks himself to be is always of the greatest importance both for what he wants to be in his life and for what he expresses in his practical reality.

Indeed it seems to be quite natural that man should look on himself as a mere genus within the class of the mammals, as there are so many bodily resemblances between himself and that class that the kinship is hardly to be denied. This kinship is of course no new discovery, but was quite well known to antiquity, although not so exactly as in our time, which has seen so much biological research. These facts are so obvious that there must have been other facts of tremendous weight which had already led in ancient times, particularly among the Greeks, to a conception of man which gave him a place outside and opposed to the rest of nature. And indeed there are such facts, and they are quite as compelling in our day as they were then. Whilst man physically is akin to the animals, he is spiritually so different that one may ask whether there is any justification in speaking of a spiritual element within animal nature at all. If by spirit we understand that element in man which manifests itself in the production of civilized cultural life, and if by culture we understand what man creates and forms beyond the region of what is biologically necessary to him, we could state, without fear of serious contradiction, that man alone has spirit, for it is he alone who creates culture. Animals do not enquire into the nature of truth for truth's sake, animals do not create new things to express in them their spirit, animals do not produce art from joy in beauty, animals do not build universities, nor temples, they do not worship the holy for the sake of holiness. While we should not deny that animals have a certain kind of intellect and also some technique based upon it, all their intellectual powers are entirely bound by their natural instinct of self-preservation of the species. Any trace of culture, of spiritual creation as the expression of non-biological spiritual impulses, like interest for truth, for beauty, for goodness and holiness, we cannot discover within their range.

53

He who for the first time steps out of the two great corridors of the British Museum, where the Egyptian and Assyrio-Babylonian sculptures are exhibited, and enters the third corridor, facing at once the figures of the Parthenon frieze, may well experience something of what Greek humanity signifies in world history: the liberation of the figure of man from the figure of the animal, the discovery of the specifically human and its principle, the spirit or *Logos* or *Nous* or Reason or whatever it may be called. What in Greek culture, in Greek art and science was an elementary experience, the philosophers, and pre-eminently Plato, have expressed in conceptions of incomparable clarity and depth and passed on to humanity as an imperishable treasure of knowledge, ideas which mankind can never forget without losing itself. Man does not live in order to live, he wants to know why and for what he lives, he feels obliged to account for the kind of life he lives. He is not required to follow the impulse of his natural instincts blindly like the animals. He can rise above these instincts, can seek truth without bothering about its usefulness. He can create the beautiful, which he has never seen, he can seek the good, which requires from him sacrifices of well-being, perhaps even the sacrifice of his life. Man does not know merely what is, but what ought to be. His mind is not satisfied with adaptation to his surroundings and its conditions and with providing only what is necessary. He cannot help looking out for an eternal meaning and an eternal reason or ground of everything. He knows not only things which are useful or hurtful for him or his species, but he also knows a divine order in all things, a law of truth, beauty, goodness. He recognizes not only that there is something, but that something ought to be. He not only sees a reality but tries to see a meaning for what is real. The Greeks comprehended all this in the gravely significant word *Logos*. By *Logos* they understood, first of all, significant speech, and in it the principle of all meaning and reasoning. Man therefore is not merely a natural being but a bearer of *Logos*. There is in him not merely a natural urge and power but a divine principle, disclosing in him the eternal meaning of law. By his thinking, by his understanding of the divine meaning, or *Logos*, or order, man participates in the divine mind, in the world-*Logos* which permeates the universe as the ordering principle which gives it meaning and makes it into a cosmos. Reason or spirit, which elevates man above the animal, at the same time ties him to the divine and in the depth of his being makes him one with it.

This is the fundamental idea of idealistic philosophy, which since the days of Plato has not ceased to inspire men and to move them to high things. There is something of deep inspiration and enchantment, and at the same time of earnest obligation and reverence, in this understanding of man as the bearer of the divine *Logos*. It is not for nothing that Plato in his *Phaidros* points to enthusiasm, divine inspiration, as the foundation of all true philosophy. But man is clearly not capable of living permanently in this enthusiasm. Somehow this high conception of man seems to be in contradiction with everyday reality. Important as may be the element of truth in this doctrine, it does not stand the serious test of reality, but appears to be a half-truth which leads of necessity to illusion. True, it is very dangerous, as we saw during the war years, if man looks on himself as an animal, for then he becomes an animal, or beast, and the most dangerous of all. But it is not less dangerous if he considers himself to be a divine being, for then he makes illusions for himself about the limits of his being, and does not see the danger which lies within him. The naturalistic conception of man, emerging as it does from a one-sided consideration of biological facts and relations, robs man of his dignity and gives him the feeling of the casualness and nothingness of his being. The idealistic conception of man on the other hand, emerging from a one-sided consideration of the spiritual element and the normative relations in his being, may make man haughty and conceal from him the problematic nature of his being. Man is neither beast nor God, and this middle thing which he is, and how he is this middle thing, cannot be deduced from general principles. Here we have reached the point where the Christian interpretation of man's existence is bound to be taken seriously.

The first sentence of the Christian doctrine of man is: Man is a creature. By this it is said that he is not God, but created by and entirely dependent upon God. Godhead, divine being, belongs (as we have seen in our last lecture) to God alone. There are only two kinds of being, divine being, God's monopoly, and creaturely being. There is no intermediate being between the two.

56

All paganism consists in asserting a continuity between the divine and the creature, or negatively in the non-acknowledgment of the absolute barrier which separates divine being from creaturely being. I alone am God, that is the fundamental statement of all biblical revelation. It is true, man is a creature of a particular kind and he has an outstanding position within that which God has created. But that does not change this fundamental statement, that he, like everything else, is a creature. The most obvious expression of his creatureliness is his body. By our body we are placed at a certain spot in this spatio-temporal world. We are here, not there, we are now, not then, we are limited. The second clear indication of this creatureliness is our being many. We are not one, as God is, but we are many. And each one of us limits the other one. This multiplicity in its various parts is manifested most clearly in individuality. Each one of us is unlike every other one. No unity of knowledge and will or feeling can remove this individuality and the insurmountable barrier which it presents.

These assertions, which seem incontrovertible, acquire their proper significance only when we assert, further, that man is a creature of a unique kind amongst the others. To express this uniqueness, and its foundation, the Bible uses a simile, a parable: man, it is said, and man alone, is created in the image of God. It is in this concept that everything is included, what we may call Christian humanism in distinction from idealistic humanism. What does this parable mean? First, obviously a similarity between the divine being and the human, and thus something which seems to be similar to that idealistic thought of man as the bearer of the divine *Logos*. But, looked at more closely, the biblical concept of the *imago dei* says something quite different. For however great and important may be the similarity between God and man, it rests on an absolute dissimilarity, namely that God is the Creator and man his creature, that God alone has independent autonomous self-originating being, whilst man's being is dependent and relative. It is only within this absolute dissimilarity that there can be any question of man's peculiar similarity to God. In the course of Christian theology this similarity expressed as the image of God has been interpreted differently, and this is not surprising, because the Bible does not speak about this point very explicitly or quite uniformly. The conception of the *imago dei* belongs, as others, such as that of history, to those elements of biblical doctrine which we have to understand more between the lines than in the lines themselves, that is to say, we have to get it out of the totality of biblical teaching. The testimony of Scripture about what is peculiar to man alone is not obscure. Man alone is created in such a way that he can and that he ought to receive God's word and live in communion with him. What makes man a man? Man's humanity consists not so much, or not in the first place, in the fact that he can think, that he can rise above the sense-world by conceptions and ideas, that by his spirit he can comprehend nature and dominate it. All that is not in itself human, but it is instrumental, that is, what is truly human is man's being a creature of such a kind that God can talk to him, and that he can and must reply. More, that all the time, in whatever he does or does not, thinks or does not think, wills or does not will, he answers God's call. God's call then is always the first thing, that which makes possible man's humanity, man's ability to answer. Man is created in such a way that a definite answer is expected from him. The kernel of man's being is responsibility, and responsibility is the essence of humanity.

This is the distinction between Greek idealistic humanism and Christian humanism. In the Christian concept man is not the bearer of the divine *Logos* and participant in divine being. What is unique in his being is not something which he has in himself but a relation which gives him life and destiny. It is not the spirit or reason which makes man the image of God, but it is his responsibility over against the Creator and his destiny to enter into communion with God. This is the essence of man's personality as distinct from everything else: the destiny of communion with God, whose very being is communion, namely love. Therefore it is not reason, not creative spirit which is the truly human element, but love, to which all creativity and thinking are subordinated. Therefore man cannot in himself or by himself be truly human, but only in communion—in communion with God, the God of love, and in itself love means communion with man.

But now the opposition between this Christian conception and the idealistic conception of man does not consist merely in this relation between God and man, as the content of the image of God, but also, secondly, in the doctrine that man in his reality is in contradiction to the will of God and to his own destiny and being. This is the doctrine of sin. Of course, Greek thinkers know something of moral evil, as do the idealists of more recent times. Kant in his doctrine of radical evil has given a picture of human reality which is anything but inspiring or elevating. No serious interpreter of human nature can overlook this dark side of human reality. Neither Plato nor his followers have simply identified real man with the divine idea of man. But when they tried to account for this difference or opposition between the idea of man and his reality, they did not find any other reason for it than his animal nature. That seemed to be the solution of the problem and riddle of man: that man is not merely spirit but also an animal with his instincts. Experience seemed to corroborate this explanation. Is it not this animal instinct which degrades man, which diverts him from the line of his destiny and brings opposition and strife and fighting into human relations? Therefore it must be the real task of human education and endeavour to free oneself from the domination of these animal instincts.

This conception of evil remains, however, on the surface and does not do justice to the dismal sinister phenomenon of evil. This character of the dismal, which is inherent in moral evil, is not due to sensual animal nature, but has its origin and its seat in the spirit. If we start from Greek or idealistic presuppositions, this cannot be understood. How should *Logos* be antilogical and spirit antispiritual? But it can be understood, if we start from the biblical idea of the image of God. If man has his true humanity in his relation to God, namely in that he acknowledges his responsibility to the Creator and that he lives in the communion to which he is called, it is possible at any time that man may find this freedom, grounded in responsibility, to be too little and that instead of being free in God, he wants to be free from God. Instead of taking his life out of the hand of God in obedience, thankfulness and trust, man can fall upon the idea to take his life into his own hands and to create what pleases him. Thanks to those gifts which the Creator has given him, man can emancipate himself from his Creator and make himself his own lord. That is what the Bible calls sin. We see at once that this has nothing to do with animal nature, but has a purely spiritual origin. Evil, understood like this, is much more dangerous, much more profound and alarming, than what idealistic philosophy conceives as evil.

The centre, then, of this phenomenon of evil is that man wants to be his own god. In modern times this nature of evil has come to the fore clearer than ever in the doctrines of two great thinkers of the last century, those two thinkers whose influence on our generation has been greater than that of anybody else—Karl Marx and Frederic Nietzsche. Marx started from the saying: 'Man can be free only if he owes his life to himself.' Therefore the real fall of man is the acknowledgment of a God upon whom man thinks himself dependent. Either freedom or faith. Nietzsche in his turn makes his

Zarathustra ask: 'If there were gods who can endure not being a god? Therefore there are no gods.' Man does not want to have somebody above him. These are the two classic new coinings of that aboriginal word of the serpent in paradise, with which it seduced man: 'You shall be like God.' It is not in the sensual animal nature of man's constitution that the origin of evil lies, but in his will to break down the barrier of creaturely relative freedom and substitute for it divine absolute freedom. Sin has its origin in a will, in a conception of freedom dictated by *hubris*. Just as the *imago dei* lies not in something constitutional or substantial, but in a relation to the Creator, so also the evil is not founded or grounded in some element of his natural constitution, but again in his relation to God, namely, in the negation of the God-given destiny and frame of man's life.

Evil understood in that fashion as sin is therefore neither an unfortunate combination of elements in human nature nor a consequence of the finality and limitations of his being; but evil is understood as a deed, an act of mind, a rebellion of the creature against the Creator, the distrust and ingratitude of the creature, to which it does not seem enough to receive freedom and life, but which believes itself to be free only if it leads its own life and is its own lord. By this attempt to emancipate himself from the divine dependence, man entangles himself in a desperate incurable contradiction of his being. He is not God, but wants to be God. Being free within God he becomes a slave by denying his dependence upon God. He is so destined and so created as to have a God; but in turning his back on God and wanting to be his own god, it comes about that without his will and knowledge the world becomes his god. And now, secondarily, not primarily, his sensual nature becomes a source of evil desire. It is not sensuality which poisons the spirit, but it is the spirit which poisons his animal nature. And now when this has happened this perverted sensuality becomes a master instead of being a tool. That is one effect of the Fall. The other is more direct: it is selfishness. Man, making himself God, wants to be the one whom everybody and every being has to serve. Having despised the love of God as the principle of his life and of his freedom, love of himself becomes the all-dominating motive. As every man wants to be his own lord and therefore wants all the others to be his servants, it is inevitable that a fight for domination should arise and become the main trait of human history.

Up to now we have spoken of evil which lies as a possibility within man created in the image of God. Man can emancipate himself from God. This freedom lies within his responsibility which can realize itself only in free decision. But now biblical doctrine goes further: it does not merely say that man *can* sin, but that man *has become* a sinner. Not this or that man, but man as such. This is the content of the idea of the Fall. Genesis iii. does not mean to tell a story, but to point to a fact: such is the situation of man, who followed the voice of seduction. Why he mistrusted God, why man chose this false freedom, the Bible does not say. That is the incomprehensible, irrational mystery of human reality.

63

Whoever seeks to explain sin, or believes that he can, makes of sin a fate and abolishes the act. The biblical concept of sin is that it is an irrational deed.

But now two other assertions are made about this act, not in order to explain it, but to show its uncanny greatness. The first of these assertions refers to the totality of man in his sin. The second refers to the totality and unity of all men in sin. Let me first try to explain in a few words the meaning of these two assertions. The first, concerning the totality of man in his sin, is not difficult or surprising after what has been said in distinction from the idealistic conception of evil. Whilst Greek idealistic thought tried to find the solution of the problem by referring it to the two elements of the natural constitution of man, his being not merely spirit, but also animal, the Bible rejects this conception as an insult to the good creation of God and as a false exoneration of man. It is not a part, an element, of human nature which is responsible for evil, but the whole man. So it is not a part of man only that is involved in evil, but again the whole man. Where responsibility of man to God is concerned, there are no parts of human nature, but there is only one person in its totality, called in its totality into the service of God.

Therefore it is not a part of man but the whole man who turns his back on God and seeks his autonomy. It is only as an effect of sin that there comes about a contradiction between spirit and body, between the animal functions and spiritual acts, a dissociation of the higher and the lower part of our nature. We do not merely sin, but we are sinners. It is not a particularly bad part of our nature which does not obey God's will, but it is our self in the oneness and totality of our person which is involved in this contradiction. All this does not mean that nothing is left of divine creation in man's nature, that man, so to say, consists of sin. The expression, 'the total depravity of man,' which in later Calvinism has become a slogan, is not biblical. But the truth of this concept is that it is the totality of man, not a part of him, which is responsible for sin. Sin is my sin. We may speak of traits of character as more or less independent centres or systems but sin is not a trait of character and therefore not divisible. To be a sinner is an indivisible unity and totality, like being a self.

With that we have come already to the second assertion concerning the solidarity of all men in sin, or the totality of mankind as sinful. This point is much more difficult and I do not know whether I shall succeed in making it clear. The Bible has represented this unity in Adam, the first man. But the content of biblical doctrine is not tied to this mythical story of Adam. What it wants to say is, first, that as the individual man being a sinner is a unity, so also the whole of humanity is a unity in its sin. That does not mean only that all men are sinners. Of course this is true and no one sincerely contests it, where the existence of sin as such is acknowledged. But the expression means something deeper, namely, that men in their sin stand in an indissoluble connexion. To give a parable, it is like the individual strawberry plants which underneath the surface are tied up with each other in a texture of roots; so individual men in their sin are somehow connected with each other under the surface of rational experience. There is a solidarity in mankind both in being created in the image of God and also in sin. No man can be violated without all the others being violated with him in his person. It belongs to the being of man that each individual man is not merely this individual man, nor merely an example of a species, but everyone is in an incomparable unique way also the whole of humanity. The most recent psychological knowledge comes near to this mysterious fact by its concept of a collective subconsciousness. I would not say that this is the thing which the Christian means, but at any rate it is a manifestation of what the Christian doctrine expresses in its paradoxical concept of original sin. In pronouncing this word we shall however bear in mind that nowhere does the Bible use the biological category of heredity or hereditary sin. Heredity is a biological concept, which does not reach into the depths of the truly personal, and if applied to sin it must lead to a fatal determinism and naturalism, which are completely foreign to biblical thought.

When we say that man not merely does sin, but is a sinner, and that humanity as a whole is a sinful humanity, the little word 'is' has a different meaning from what it has in such a sentence as 'This man is a negro'. Man is a sinner means that he is a kind of being which, while inescapably given, is at the same time not without responsibility. Sin is both an act and a condition, an act which lies behind us and a being or condition manifesting itself in acts.

It is evident that we are here touching a limit of our understanding; we are trying to formulate an experience of faith which we cannot express in thought without contradiction. But this is the experience: sin is a deed for which we are responsible, and sin is our being which we are unable to get out of. If we are placed before God, we know that it is so, although we cannot comprehend why it is so. I know I am myself responsible for my sin and cannot put the blame on God's creation. But at the same time my sin, which also is the sin of everyone else, is something from which I cannot disentangle myself. I cannot make myself such a one as I know I ought to be, or as I am destined to be by divine creation. I am a fallen creature, prisoner of his own godlessness. And I am this as member of a fallen humanity. No moral or religious endeavour or exertion can get me out of this condition, just because it is I myself who am affected by sin, not merely a part of me.

This whole knowledge, both of our creation in the image of God and of our sin, we cannot gain by psychological introspection. It is part of the nature of sin that it darkens our view, that we always try to excuse ourselves. We do that in one of two ways: we acknowledge our inability not to sin, but we explain it as a natural fact in a deterministic manner. We say, 'I cannot help it', and mean by that, 'I am not responsible.' Or we try to explain sin in some such attenuating manner as we have seen in the Greek concept or by recognizing deeds as simply evil without acknowledging the existence of sinful being. The knowledge of sin comes to us in faith. It is knowledge gained in the act of revelation in Christ. We shall speak more of this in the following lecture. But whilst this knowledge can be gained only by faith, it certainly does not contradict, but it exactly coincides with natural psychology, experience with ourselves and other men.

The picture of man which we gain in our own life and in the history of humanity is a thoroughly mysterious and contradictory one. It bears the mark of that contradiction which Pascal put in that famous formula 'Grandeur et misère de l'homme' and which he elaborated in a picture of incomparable realism and psychological sharpness as the picture of the real man. This real man is always and everywhere God's image, yet rebelling against him. He is a being in permanent conflict with himself, with God and with his fellows. This *roi dépossédé*, who is responsible to God and yet defies God, can never forget that he was destined for the highest, yet constantly misses his destiny. This man in revolt, who earnestly longs to emerge from it, nevertheless renews that revolt again and again.

Whether we are concerned with the psychology of the individual or with great historical movements or with social and cultural phenomena, we find this conflict everywhere. It is not true, as William James led us to believe, that there are two kinds of men, the harmonious ones and the split ones. Certainly there are considerable differences along these lines. But even the harmonious ones are sinners, living in conflict with their destiny and contradiction of it, whether they know it or not. And also the so-called sick souls are not sick as compared with the healthy, but are rather the ones who see what their own and everyone's condition is.

In closing, let me ask a question which arises from the last observation. What meaning or importance has it, whether a man sees and understands himself in one way or another? This question can be answered on two different levels. The recent terrible years of the world war and of the preceding totalitarian revolutions have shown us that the understanding of man is the basis of all social order and of all culture. The acknowledgment of a human dignity which is not from man but is bestowed by God is the presupposition of all political and social justice and freedom. The denial of this dignity is equivalent to the total abandonment of man to the power of the state and is in principle identical with the principle of the totalitarian states. The totalitarian state can arise, and is bound to arise, wherever the idea of human dignity has been lost. The idea of human dignity, however, is historically and in principle none other than the idea of man's being created in the image of God.

It seems possible to understand the dignity of man in an idealistic instead of in the Christian sense. It was Stoic philosophy which, before Christianity had entered the plane of history, had done so much for the creation of western law and justice. But this idealist conception of man has come to grief again and again on the real facts of human life and has on the other hand done much harm by its abstract egalitarianism. You cannot make man believe for any length of time that he is a divine being; he knows, even if he is not a Christian, too much of that 'misère d'homme' to be able to take the enthusiastic idealist interpretation seriously. That is why a time of idealism has always been followed by one of materialism in which human dignity was denied. Such was the case after the idealist tide of the nineteenth century, which was followed by a terrible ebb of crudest materialism, which had nothing else to say of man but that he was the most differentiated and developed animal.

In quite recent times we seem to have entered a particularly dangerous phase of anthropological aberration, namely a queer combination of nihilism and deification. Theoretically man is said to be nothing but an animal with a highly developed cerebrum. At the same time it is believed of this man that he is capable by science and technical devices of achieving whatever he wants. The deification which might have been thought to be finally overcome, returns as it were from behind, in the form of a deification of technical creativity to which not much less than omnipotence is ascribed. After mankind has done away with the pseudo-religion of race and blood, it is faced with the even greater danger of a technocratical pseudo-religion. There is no room for human personality, freedom and justice in either of these new religions of divine man. But the most dangerous of all must be the one which makes man at the same time nothing and God.

There is only one way out of this miserable pendulum movement between negation of all human dignity and unmeasured exaggeration of his divinity, namely, the Christian knowledge which sees man's greatness and

70

misery together in a way which is in line with experience. This realistic doctrine of man, which acknowledges the image of God as well as the depth of sin, is able to create a social order which has room for the dignity of man and at the same time provides for the necessary precautions against the terrible forces of evil which are slumbering in man. Such is the view of the problem from outside, from the sphere of public life.

But it is one of the most harmful aberrations of our time that it gives far too high an importance to public life, and has forgotten that the truly human is not to be found in public, but in the private and intimate sphere of human life. In previous times people knew the difference between the temporal and the eternal and they knew that all political and social order, however important it may be, belongs to the sphere of temporal things. States and social orders, the good ones and the bad ones, will one day be no more. But man is created for eternity and therefore his relation to the eternal is the central and in the last analysis the only decisive question of his existence. In distinction from Greek idealism this has been made known to us by the Christian message, and it is knowledge which is inseparably united with the knowledge of what man is. That he is created in God's image means that he is created for eternity; that he is a sinner means that he has failed to achieve his destiny. His grandeur, to speak once more with Pascal, is that he is destined for communion with God; his misery is his separation from God and thereby his separation from the source of eternal life. If we ask what there is of importance in the Christian doctrine of man, the answer must be: that by it alone man knows what he is created for, what, therefore, the meaning of his life is. By it alone he knows what his reality is. And this reality is of such a kind that he must despair, if something new does not happen to him. The knowledge which through faith we have of our reality is indeed knowledge of despair, but this despair is the only possible avenue to the saving knowledge which is given to us in the message of Jesus Christ. The acknowledgment that I am a sinner, incapable of being not a sinner and becoming again that for which I am destined, is the entrance to God's saving grace, in which Christian faith and the salvation of the world consist.

IV

The Mediator

IT is a well-known fact which every preacher and pastor can confirm, that many, even of those who are related to the Christian church, believe in God, but do not believe in Jesus Christ. God to them is a reality without which they cannot conceive their lives to exist. But the message of the New Testament, of Jesus Christ, the Son of God, our Lord, is incomprehensible to them. It has no real meaning. And particularly foreign to them is the idea of the death of Jesus on the cross having the meaning of a reconciling sacrifice. This 'Pauline idea', as it is often called, is to them nothing but the remains of a primitive conception of God as a revengeful bloodthirsty being whose wrath can be appeased only by a blood sacrifice. What is the reason for this estrangement from the centre of the biblical message?

If we want to find the right answer it is necessary to point to a characteristic trait of modern spiritual evolution which has long been observed in other connexions, namely, the depersonalization of modern life and understanding of life. No doubt the idea of personality and personal life plays a large part in the thought of modern thinkers, but an analysis of this conception of personality would show that modern man, when he speaks of person and the personal, has in mind something which ultimately is quite impersonal, namely, a function within society or culture. He thinks of the creative genius and his work, he thinks of the role which a certain individual plays within a certain sphere of life. He thinks of a certain man contributing to the common stock of civilization. Very often you can observe that most people of our generation cannot distinguish between personality and individuality. What personality is in the strict absolute sense can be understood only in confrontation with the personal God. It is the biblical, particularly the New Testament gospel, from which humanity has learned and can alone learn what 'person' and 'personal' mean. No philosophical theism, but only the revelation of the personal God, can tell us the meaning of a personal God, and therefore the meaning of human personality.

It is by the incomprehensible miracle of divine revelation that we are enabled to know that God, the Creator of the whole universe, and the Lord of all nations, looks upon me, this individual man, and wants to have communion with me, this individual; that he knows me and loves me, that he has elected me—me, and not mankind in general—before all eternity in Jesus Christ. Therefore he is not concerned in the first place about the work I am producing, about the social function I am fulfilling, about the role in society I am playing, but he is primarily concerned about one thing, whether or not I love him with all my heart and all my powers, 'for the Lord looketh on the heart.' The heart, however, is the person.

More, by the fact that 'God looketh on thy heart' and calls me into communion with him, I become in the true sense of the word a person. A genius, a talented or important personality, a well-defined individuality, a character of a certain stamp—all that I can be without this relation to God; but I am a person only 'in the face of God.'

It is of decisive importance for the understanding of our topic that we clearly see the difference between a divine will which aims at unity, and a divine will which aims at community. The God of revelation purposes communion, not unity, the God of mysticism and of philosophical speculation purposes unity, not communion. Unity makes for the impersonal, community for the personal, because God wants communion and in his will to communion his own deepest being, his Trinity, manifests itself. The ultimate word which the Bible speaks is love. God is love. That does not mean only that God loves, but that love is his essence. This is the mystery of the triune God, that his own being is communion. He is in himself the loving and the beloved. That is why love is his ultimate word to us, and because this is his ultimate word, personality in the deep true sense of the word is possible and this personality has unconditional supremacy over everything impersonal.

On the other hand that is why sin is not merely the transgression of a divine law, the destruction of an order which God has established and sustained. These things are true of sin, but they are not sin itself. Sin is the destruction of communion with God, the dissolution of the personal link which holds God and man together. This is the reason why sin is far beyond the realm of morality. 'Against thee only have I sinned and done that which is evil in thy sight.' Sin is not that I have done something wrong, sin is that I have separated myself from God. That is what is meant when somebody says, 'I am a sinner.' To what was expounded about sin in the previous lecture we have therefore to add another aspect, which is expressed in the word 'guilt' of sin. For sin is the destruction of personal communion with God and, as such, is a fact which we ourselves cannot alter. Even if we had the power to sin no more, and if we had the possibility of repairing the damage which has been caused by sin, there would still remain something which we could not repair, namely, guilt, the fact that we are separated from God. The gate of paradise has been closed; before it stands the Cherub with the flaming sword, not allowing us to return. The tie of communion with God is torn and cannot, so far as we are concerned, be retied, we have no power over that which is past, as past it stands between God and us like a wall separating us.

And now we remember what has been said in our second lecture about the essence of the living God who is revealed to us, that he is not merely the loving but also the holy God. God takes himself seriously. That is why he can take us seriously, for 'God is not mocked, whatsoever a man soweth that shall he reap.' He who has separated himself from God *is* separated from him, between him and God there stands guilt as a reality, which is acknowledged also by God. The living God is not, as the philosophers say, unchangeable, simply, but his attitude towards us does change. Because we have stepped out of the position in which his creation had placed us, his disposition towards us is no longer what it was in the beginning. This changed disposition caused by the rupture of communion through sin is called in the Bible the wrath of God.

This word sounds unbearably harsh in the ear of modern man. He sees in it nothing but a primitive crude anthropomorphism. Even human wrath seems to him as a reaction to an offence to be unworthy of a spiritual man. How much more unworthy of God! But it is not mere chance, nor is it a matter of slow evolution, that this concept plays such a large part not only in the Old Testament but even in the New. If we understand it properly it has nothing whatever to do with primitiveness, with naive anthropomorphism. On the contrary, it is the necessary expression of God, taking himself and us seriously. He takes us so seriously that our changed attitude with regard to him produces a change in his attitude towards us. If it were not so it would mean that our action, our disposition, is nothing to God and that would mean that we are nothing to him, that he does not love us. Furthermore it would mean that 'God *is* mocked', that he does not take his own command and will seriously, that he is not unyielding, unbendable and that he is therefore not reliable. The term 'God's wrath' therefore means that the breach of communion, which has been made from our side, means also a breach for

God. It means that our guilt is guilt in his sight too, that our separation from him is a reality for him too, that his holy will, encountering resistance, becomes in itself resistance: 'God resisteth the haughty.' God's law must not be broken; if we do break it, it will break us.

Behind the idea of guilt, therefore, stands the idea of judgment, punishment and condemnation. These too are words which modern man in his impersonal thinking cannot stand. Impersonality becomes sentimentality and at the same time arrogance. Just as our penal law and its concept of punishment has become sentimental and impersonal, watered down by mere ideas of utility, so in religion the thought of divine punishment, judgment and condemnation has been off-hand abolished. One speaks of an irreligious use of juridical categories within the Bible, but does not acknowledge that the conception of holiness has its own place apart from love. One wants to have love alone, not seeing that by denying God's holiness and wrath, God's love is deprived of its true depth and meaning. Is it not so even in human experience? The man who cannot become angry, cannot truly love. The man who passes over treachery, infidelity, breach of confidence as if it were nothing, cannot be a true friend and cannot be faithful himself. It is here that a decision of the first order takes place: he who refuses to hear of God's wrath, judgment and condemnation, will never understand Jesus Christ. The living God is the God whose love is united with holiness. This paradox of holiness and mercy is, as we have already seen, the essence of the biblical doctrine of God.

Perhaps it is of less importance whether in this connexion we speak of the holiness of God or of his righteousness, but it is certainly not unimportant that the concept
of the holiness of God is not simply replaced by that
of righteousness or justice, because holiness goes deeper
than what is ordinarily understood by divine righteousness or justice. The biblical phrase 'the righteousness of
God' is so comprehensive in its meaning that we cannot
reproduce it in any modern language without an exten-
sive periphrasis. It is in God's being holy that his justice
or righteousness towards us is established, if by justice
we understand what everybody in our day understands
by justice. The holiness of God consists in God's willing
himself unconditionally, in his desiring to be God and
Lord alone, in his not yielding his honour to anyone,
but desiring to have the world filled with his glory.
Out of this holiness springs his wrath, his resistance
against the one who resists him. Out of his holiness comes
the necessity of judgment and punishment for the one
who separates himself from God and turns his back
upon him. The holiness of God is, if I may use such
human terms, the infinite divine self-respect, without
which his love would not be divine love, but sentimentality. It is the love of the holy God which is the miracle
revealed in the Bible. Upon this holiness of God therefore is grounded the fact that the breach of communion
which is sin is a reality for God also, and this is expressed
by God's reaction in holy wrath. Man as sinner stands
under the divine judgment, he has nothing to expect
but the consequences of his doings, namely, reprobation.

This is the effect of that estrangement in which he has placed himself.

But we know that this is not God's last word. We enter the innermost sanctuary of divine revelation, the mystery of divine forgiveness: 'God wishes not the death of the sinner, but that he repent!' The wrath of God is a reality, but the wrath of God is not God's essence. Scripture says that God is love, but never that God is wrath. This is the incomprehensible mystery of the divine essence, that God's holiness is perfected in his love, although it is not interchangeable with it. The wall of partition, which now stands between God and man as the consequence of sin, is a reality for God as well, but it is not the ultimate reality. We must not deny its reality because it is not ultimate, but on the other hand we must not doubt the divine mercy because of the reality of the wrath. This in a few words is the meaning of the message of the cross of Jesus Christ.

The word of divine mercy, which is divine forgiveness, is the most precious word of all because in it the word of God's love takes on a new unfathomable and inexhaustible meaning. It is exactly for that reason that this most precious word of all must be guarded from the most terrible danger, that the miracle of mercy and forgiveness shall become a matter of course. We have already quoted the blasphemous words of the mocker: 'Dieu pardonnera, c'est son métier!' In these words the terrible thing happens that sinful man regards divine forgiveness as a matter of course, as something which he can deduce from a preconception of God. Everything which tends to trivialize the miracle of forgiveness or change it into a bagatelle or a matter of course is evil and abominable. And everything which tends to make us see the miracle of forgiveness as an incomprehensible miracle, as something which could never be expected, is good and necessary. God himself has provided the decisive safeguard. The cross of Jesus Christ is that event, within divine revelation, by which it is made impossible for us to take divine forgiveness lightly. This is the deepest reason why the message of the cross is foolishness to the Greeks and a stumbling-block for the Jews. The message of the cross or rather the event itself is the divine medium by which forgiveness is given the full weight of the unheard-of, the incomprehensible and, seen from man's side, the impossible. But this does not happen as it were by a divine rhetoric but by a divine inward necessity; for in the message of the cross both are revealed as one: divine holiness, which is not mocked, and divine love as the unconditional will to communion.

Let me try at the outset to remove an objection which is often heard. Since the time of the Socinians it has been said again and again that the Pauline doctrine of the cross is in contradiction to the simple message of Jesus himself as it is presented in the parable of the prodigal son. In this parable, it is said, the father forgives his son without the intervention of a mediator, without any reference to the bloody event of the cross. Furthermore, even in the Old Testament, for instance in Psalm 103, the forgiveness of God is proclaimed in the most astonishing simplicity and clarity, without any reference to an atoning sacrifice. The doctrine of reconciliation by the cross is therefore, it is said, an unnecessary complication of the simple doctrine of Jesus and at the same time a theological theory which represents a relapse into Old Testament priestly rites of atonement. It is the Jewish theologian Paul who has darkened and even falsified the Gospel of Jesus, which is so human and simple.

This conception, which mistakenly supposes itself to be the product of historical critical investigation, is in reality a completely unhistorical misunderstanding of the teaching of Jesus. The teaching of Jesus can never be separated from his person. The parable of the prodigal son is, as the context clearly shows, a commentary on what Jesus does. The Pharisees are scandalized by his intercourse with publicans and sinners. It is in replying to them and justifying his doing that he tells the parables of the prodigal son, of the lost penny, and the lost sheep or the good shepherd. It is particularly in the last one that Jesus depicts himself. He is the good shepherd who is looking for the lost sheep. He is the one who entered the house of the publican Zacchaeus and explained what he is doing in the words: 'The Son of Man is come to seek and to save that which was lost.' His whole life is this movement of coming down and entering into sinful human reality. So, too, is his imminent death, as he himself points out, a ransom for many. Even if the explicit mention in the establishment of the Lord's Supper of his blood shed for the forgiveness of sin, were not his own words, but later tradition, as many scholars are inclined to believe, there still remain that indissoluble connexion between the life and teaching of Jesus and the indisputable fact that Jesus was conscious of being the one who in God's commission restored the torn tie between God and lost man. Nor is it surprising that he himself did not say more about his coming death than the Synoptic picture of his life indicates that he said. It was not his business to preach his coming death, because such a doctrine could not be understood as long as he lived. It was his task to live and to die in the service of God and man's salvation. Therefore the opposition between Paul and Jesus is not a historical fact, but an invention of historians, who have not been able to see the unity between the two, because as modern men they did not understand this unity.

The real facts of the New Testament tradition, understood as they wish to be understood, do not allow us to separate the teaching from the life and death of Jesus Christ. In fact the most recent critical research has restored this insight to us. Jesus knew himself to be the fulfiller of Old Testament prophecy. Often enough, although as a rule more in the form of allusion corresponding to his incognito, he pointed to himself as the one in whom the coming of the kingdom of God and of the new covenant has begun, that covenant which according to the prophecy of Jeremiah is a covenant of divine forgiveness. Jesus sees his whole life as a divine act of forgiveness; through him, in him, the connexion between sinful man and the holy God which had been destroyed, is restored. That is why he came to seek what is lost. That is why his life is a service and his person a ransom for many. The consummation of this whole divine intervention in the life of Jesus is his death.

As far as the Old Testament is concerned, what is true about it in general is true in this specific question: the Old Testament is the predecessor and the foreshadowing of things to come. That is why in the Old Testament many things are separate which in the New Testament have become a unity. The king is not the priest and the prophet is neither king nor priest. It is only in the person of Christ that those three theocratic offices are united personally. Similarly we can understand that at one time, as for instance in Psalm 103, the forgiveness of God appears as detached from any atoning sacrifice. At another place, in connexion with the prophecy of the great prophet of the exile, we find the picture of the servant of God who bears vicariously the sin of his people. And again, within the context of priestly tradition, we find the idea of a vicarious atoning sacrifice. Again we must say that it is an unhistorical interpretation which takes each of these traits by itself without reference to the others.

It must also be said that, like all other doctrines of the Old Testament, even the doctrine of sin is incomplete and preliminary. But whilst this is so, it can safely be said that all these doctrines are closely linked to the divine action and revelation in history. Nowhere do we find such timeless doctrine as we find for instance in Greek philosophy or in the mystical wisdom of the Far East. Old Testament doctrine is part of Old Testament history, the doctrine being always a commentary on divine actions.

This is true in general and it is also true of forgiveness. What the psalmist says of God's forgiveness, he says on the basis of historical revelation. Psalm 103 itself, which is so often quoted in this connexion, speaks of divine forgiveness on the basis of what God has done in Israel through Moses and the prophets. It is not forgiveness deduced from a conception of God, but forgiveness which has been mercifully revealed in history. Forgiveness is an element within that history of God's coming to man, God's entering into, God's intervening in the human situation.

The message of the cross must not be severed from the whole of saving history (*Heilsgeschichte*). As it is false to speak of forgiveness without pointing to the cross, it is false also to isolate the cross from the rest of the life of Christ. The death of Jesus on the cross is the point of culmination or, if you like, the lowest point of divine self-manifestation in history. But it is the culmination of that total life which has not been lived merely in order to die, but in order to make visible God's glory and loving-kindness by teaching, living, and suffering. As it is a mistake to read the gospel without the commentary of the apostles, so it is also a mistake to read the doctrines of the apostles without the full story of Jesus as we find it in the gospels. If this is attempted that which belongs together is torn asunder. *Logos* and *sarx*, word and life taken together are that revelation of which the New Testament gives testimony. We cannot understand the life of Christ if we do not understand it as culminating in the cross, neither do we understand the cross if we do not understand it in connexion with the whole life of

Jesus. The cross of Christ and the message of atonement or redemption is nothing but the last phase of incarnation, which in itself is the final phase of God's coming to man. Again, incarnation is in itself the beginning of the cross and of redemption, as Paul expresses it with incomparable depth and simplicity in one verse in his *Epistle to the Philippians*, speaking of Jesus Christ, 'Who, being in the form of God, counted it not a prize to be on an equality with God; but emptied himself, takiñg the form of a servant, being made in the likeness of men; and being found in fashion as a man, he humbled himself becoming obedient unto death, yea, the death of the cross.'

What then is the meaning of the cross understood in this wider context of the history of revelation? We have already said that it is the divine means of showing to us sinners the holiness of God together with his mercy, and of revealing forgiveness in such a way as to exclude the misunderstanding of it as being a matter of course. This is true, but this is not the whole story. Since Anselm of Canterbury and Abelard, that is to say, since the beginning of the twelfth century, there are two classical interpretations of the meaning of the cross and its redeeming power, an objective and a subjective theory. The objective, or perhaps objectivist, doctrine of Anselm tries to prove the objective necessity of the atoning death of Christ by using the concept of necessary satisfaction. God's honour demanded the sacrifice of Jesus as the only sufficient means of reconciliation. On the other hand, Abelard affirms, with the same one-sidedness, the subjective effect of the death on the cross upon man, as being the means by which man understands and believes God's incredible love. Both theories represent an important element of the biblical testimony. But each of them is not merely incomplete, but in its one-sidedness a distortion of the biblical testimony. In saying this we should emphasize that Anselm has grasped the larger half of the truth. It is true that in the teaching of the apostles about the death of Christ, the effect of that death as revealing divine love plays a large part. But this interpretation never exhausts the whole content of biblical doctrine. What gives Anselm's thought its superiority is the fact that it starts from the objective fact of guilt. Guilt is a reality, even for God. Man's revolt against God's will is a fact against which God reacts with his wrath, therefore the divine wrath is a reality and not, as many modern theologians have believed, an inferior idea, a prejudice of man which is removed or corrected by Jesus. The reality of guilt, the existence of that wall of partition, is no prejudice, it is so real and so serious that something has to be done about it, that God may reveal his forgiving love.

Perhaps we understand this best if we take our starting-point from the passage quoted from Philippians, from the fact of incarnation. As we have already said, God's whole revelation is a coming down to man. He enters man's earthly sinful history. God wants to meet man there, where he, the real man, is. The place where God can meet man is therefore determined by the situation of man. Just as somebody who wants to help us has to travel there and enter into the conditions in which we are, so God wanting to help man must enter into the curse under which the whole human life stands as a result of sin.

This curse is not merely actual misery, the sinful power-lessness of man; the curse has a greater depth than that. It is man's being under the divine wrath, man's being lost to God. The heart of the curse is that separation from God, that expulsion from communion with the Creator, that wall of partition which is established be-tween God and man and is affirmed by divine will. God himself has placed man in this position, under the curse, because he is the holy God who is not mocked. This, then, is the situation of man not merely looked upon from man's side, but also from God's. And into this situation God must enter in order to meet man.

When we say, God must, this is of course not a neces-sity imposed upon God, but a reality shown to us by God himself. It is not an *a priori* but an *a posteriori* know-ledge; it is not to be deduced from the concept of God, but is an interpretation of an historical event. It is an attempt to understand the meaning of what has really happened in the death of Christ. It is here that our way parts from that of Anselm, who thinks it possible to deduce *a priori* from his concept of God the fact of reconciliation. It is this *a priori* construction which gives his doctrine the fatal trait of rational calculation, which makes this theory look not merely strange but also sin-ister. In this connexion I should like to point out one thing more. We agree with Anselm that there is an objective necessity in reconciliation. But we completely disagree with him if he thinks of this reconciliation as being a sacrifice by which God's wrath has to be appeased. In biblical testimony God is never the object of reconciliation; nowhere do we find this idea, that God has to be reconciled by Christ. God is always the subject of reconciliation. He reconciles man to himself. It is at this point that post-Reformation doctrine, following Anselm, has passed beyond biblical testimony and has caused the misunderstanding that the Christian doctrine of atonement is a relapse into primitive sacrificial mythology. We remain strictly in line with biblical testimony if on the one hand we underline the objectivity of divine wrath and of the curse laid upon humanity, and on the other hand emphasize that by the death of Christ the reality of divine wrath has been removed, but that God is the subject and not the object of this reconciling action.

This seems to be an impossible contradiction, as long as we do not understand the relation between divine holiness and love. As we have already said, God's wrath is an effect of his holiness, but it does not belong to his essence; on the other hand, God's holiness is not identical with his love, but his holy will finds its complete fulfilment in the realization of love. Therefore it is God's love which gives rise to the whole history of revelation, and it is God's love which leads to the cross of the Saviour. This love, however, is revealed in such a way that at the same time God's holiness in its inexorable severity becomes manifest. This is what Paul has welded together in his concept of *dikaiosunē theou*, the righteousness of God. The revelation of God's righteousness, which is opposed to the righteousness of the law, is nothing but the unity of God's judging holiness and God's reconciling merciful love. It is this righteousness of God, combining justice and mercy, to which justification by faith corresponds. And this is the new principle of life in the Christian community.

I am quite aware of the fact that in what I have been saying I have introduced you into a sphere of difficult theological conceptions, but I dare to entertain the hope that what I said at the beginning may have been sufficient to give you the impression that these things are not abstract, academic theology. In the New Testament, even in the most difficult parts of Paul's letters, there is nothing which has no immediate relation to our practical situation and problems. Here where we are concerned with the centre of the biblical message, we are concerned also with the centre of our life's problem. This centre is not what we call the social problem, much less the political, urgent and burning as these questions are. The centre is nothing else but man himself, the person, the heart of man. When they brought to Jesus a man stricken with incurable paralysis, that he might heal him, he said, to the astonishment and probably to the disappointment of most, not, 'Stand up and be healed', but, 'Son, thy sins are forgiven thee'. I think that most modern men reading this story go through the same experience as those who were present then. To us the most urgent and important thing that needs doing does not seem to be forgiveness of sin, but the cure of our practical needs. Jesus, however, sees deeper than we, whilst we in our generation are perhaps even further from the true sight of man than the time of Jesus. In distinction from previous times, the problem of guilt does not seem to be real to most of our contemporaries and many do not understand at all how man can feel guilty with regard to God.

But we should not take our direction from the short-sightedness and superficiality of our generation, but from the depth-searching vision of Jesus. He knows, he says, and he confirms by his cross, that the problem of guilt is the centre of all human predicament and perplexity. Whether we understand it or not, believe it or not, it is so all the same: because men do not have communion with God, they are living in fear, they are looking for life where there is death, and they are fleeing from that which would be life. Because he does not live in community with God, man becomes impersonal, abstract, dissociated, and succumbs to the dangerous idolatries of abstract powers. When the other day I was asked what was the real trouble with the German nation and the real cause of its corruption, I replied, without much reflection, 'Abstraction'. Perhaps I should have added, 'But that abstraction is also, perhaps in a lesser degree, the evil of all western civilization.' The specific evil of the modern history of thought, the most apparent symptom of this abstraction, is the fact that modern man does not understand guilt, that the problem of guilt hardly interests him, with the exception perhaps of the guilt of war, that is, where he is not guilty himself.

Guilt is the deepest of all human needs because the kernel of man, his relation to God, his being a person, is determined by it, even when and just when he does not know it. The message of forgiveness of guilt in its New Testament form as the message of forgiveness through the atoning death of Christ is therefore the great scandal or stumbling-block for modern man, even more than for the Greek and the Jews. Even from aesthetic motives modern man—like Goethe, the great example of modern aesthetic life—says that he does not want to hear of the cross; it is just ugly. Why should he look at a criminal hanging on a gallows? But even more, it is his moral self-esteem which revolts against the cross. He does not want to hear that this had to be done for him without him, he does not want to bend his head beneath this yoke by complete humiliation. He does not want to receive, he is too proud to receive by divine mercy. It is all that against which he cannot help revolting. This self-pride of men, which Paul calls in Greek *kauchēma*, is the fundamental negative topic of the biblical message, because it is the contradiction of that complete dependence upon God which is indicated in the words 'faith' and 'the fear of God'. This self-pride is the result of self-will, of that tendency of man to be the creator of his own life. This will to owe his life to himself manifests itself most distinctly in that pride which does not want to live by grace but by man's own doings. This is what Paul calls justice, or the righteousness of the law. This self-righteousness can be truly overcome only by the message of the reconciling death of Jesus Christ. That is why this doctrine of the cross and of justification by faith, being the centre of the New Testament and the life-source of reformation, is also the centre of all true understanding of the gospel for our time, although it is necessary to formulate it in such a way that modern man feels the challenge and sees before him the choice either to revolt against the scandal or to accept thankfully and to bow humbly before the incredible mercy of God.

V

Resurrection

IN recent times there has been much talk of the contrast between the static and the dynamic, not merely in connexion with political movements, which pride themselves on the dynamic, but also in connexion with religion. Modern man seems to demand that religion be dynamic, not static. What exactly he means by that, is not always very clear. But two things seem to be implied in this word: religion must be related to the time-process, giving it direction and finality; second, religion must be what is indicated in the original meaning of the word *dunamis*, a power moving the life of men.

It is not difficult to see that the gospel of the New Testament, as distinguished from other religions, to a large extent fulfils these demands. For Christian faith has undoubtedly a relation to the time-process, giving it direction and finality, and the gospel is certainly to be understood as a power moving the life of man. Is it not the apostle Paul himself who calls the gospel of Jesus Christ a power of God unto salvation? All the same we should be cautious about applying such a pattern as the contrast between the static and the dynamic, which is at

94

man's disposal, and using it as a means of interpretation of biblical truth. If the gospel is foolishness to the world and a stumbling-block to its wisdom, as has been shown in the four preceding lectures, we can hardly expect that it will submit itself to such a pattern and postulate as that of dynamism, which is entirely drafted from man's point of view. Therefore it will be necessary to submit this supposed criterion of true religion to a severe critical examination.

At first it may do us this service, that it points to a striking contrast between religions. There are religions which have no relation, or merely a negative one, to time or the time-process, which therefore are really static. I am speaking of those religions which interpret the world as a well-ordered eternal universe, a divine cosmos, and which therefore place all the emphasis on conservation, on the stability of this order which man has to acknowledge and to respect. The most striking example of this kind of religion is probably the religion of China, which laid the foundation of a cultural and social order of unparalleled stability in that immense territory of the Far East, but which finally led to such a torpor that it could end only in catastrophe. Less outspoken, but similar in its limits, is Greek religion together with the religious philosophy that originated from it. Its main conception is that of the divine order, of a world-cosmos. The Indian religions, including mysticism of all shades, have almost an entirely negative relation to time or to temporal events. With nature-religion they share the idea that the time-process—so far as it has reality—is an eternal cyclic or circular movement in which everything recurs, and returns in longer or shorter periods of rotation.

The biblical doctrine is quite different. Here temporal events have a decisive importance, here human history is not like natural growing and vanishing, a circular movement with direction and end. On the contrary, from the very beginning, starting with that story of Abraham and the covenant between God and his people, everything is directed towards a future goal. History is thought of as the becoming of something which is not yet, but will be, which we do not yet have, but shall have. Even though this goal is all too limited and all too concretely earthly in its first presentations, nevertheless in the course of the divine history of revelation it becomes clearer and clearer that it is not some goal, but *the* end towards which this history is running. The realization of this history of revelation and its aim is not automatic; it does not take place in the natural course of events, but through powerful acts of intervention by God, in which he uses men and provides them with supernatural forces. Here then the postulate of dynamic religion seems to be fulfilled completely.

But if we analyse this postulate a little more closely, we see that behind it lies the idea of progress and perhaps that of evolution. This is the way in which modern man understands the dynamic and the positive relation to time-processes. The world shall move, be it in small steps or in big leaps, forward, more and more towards a goal. And the power which leads towards that goal, the power by which humanity is brought closer and closer to it, is that dynamic which he postulates.

I do not mean by that to imply unconditionally the idea of a continual and non-intermittent process of progression. Modern man knows that there are setbacks, good times and bad times, times when the world moves onward with big strides, and times when it reaches a standstill, and even completely loses previous gains. But however irrational may be the zigzag lines of these movements and however great the disappointment, all the same, taken as a whole we move forward and we may hope that the generations after us will see a better, more human time than we, and may have it as a permanent gain. It is undeniable that this idea of progress sprang from Christianity, and this is acknowledged by the historians. Furthermore, it cannot be denied that a large number of Christians do in their turn interpret the gospel by means of this concept of progress, some in a more evolutionary, others in a more revolutionary way. But both are unanimous in affirming that history or the time-process brings us closer and closer to the goal. We must realize, however, that, so far as Christian faith is concerned, this idea of progress is relatively new. The question of such a progress, which to us seems so self-evident, was never raised in the time of the Reformation or in the Middle Ages, or in the time of the early Church Fathers. The decisive question, however, is whether the idea of progress is known to the Bible. This question must be answered with unqualified decision in the negative. The idea of progress in all its shapes, evolutionary and revolutionary, has sprung from Christianity, but in such a way that at the same time it represents a modern rationalistic and optimistic re-coining of the biblical idea of the coming kingdom of God. The biblical message *has* a very definite and positive relation to the time-process and it does show a goal of history. Therefore it does give human existence a clear and firm direction. But in all this it is far removed from the idea of progress which lies behind the catch-word 'dynamic.' The relation which the New Testament gospel gives us to time and the temporal process is not only very different from that of progress, but it is in itself thoroughly paradoxical, that is, it is not to be grasped in the categories of our rational thought, and therefore it is foolishness and a stumbling-block to our natural way of thinking. I should like to make this clear in what follows.

Let me first point to an idea which is in the centre of the New Testament message and stands in closest connexion with that centre of which we were speaking in the last lecture, with the message of the cross. I am refering, if you will allow me to coin such a monstrous word, to the idea of *onceness*. What has happened in the cross of Christ has happened, as the apostles emphasize over and over again, once and for all. It needs no supplementing or enlarging and it does not bear repetition. The last word of Christ on the cross, according to the gospel by John is, 'It is finished,' or, in words closer to the Greek, 'It is perfected.' Perfect for ever. This idea of something completely exhaustive, sufficient for ever, is a scandal for our rational thinking and feeling. We like to have different possibilities before us in order to decide, to decide for ourselves. But here it is said, 'There is no salvation in any other, there is only this door to true life.' If we think in terms of dynamism we like to think that what is decisive is before us, that we may take part in it; here however it is said, the decision *has taken place*. You are tied, tied in an absolute sense to something which belongs to the past. Both these elements, being tied to the past and being tied to one, to the exclusion of any other, is opposed, indeed revolting, to the modern mind. It is so humiliating, so opposed to our democratic mood, and it does not correspond at all to what we understand by dynamic.

But strangely enough, this onceness does not correspond to the static either. For in this one point of history what takes place is the reversion of all history, the revolution compared with which all other revolutions are an empty noise. It is the decisive battle in the struggle between God and the godless powers. As Paul depicts it in his Epistle to the Colossians in a grandiose and dramatic picture, 'Having put off from himself the principalities and the powers, he made a show of them openly, triumphing over them in it (the cross).' It is the picture of a victorious Roman general returning triumphantly at the head of his army, followed by the prisoners carrying the spoils, and entering through the *porta triumphalis*. Just as the allied troops after D-day, after the invasion of the Continent had been successful, knew that the victory was theirs, even when there lay before them long days and even months of fighting; so Christians, since the

D-day of Christ, since the great invasion of the kingdom of God into our history had succeeded and the decisive battle had been fought on the cross, knew that victory was theirs, even when there lay before them long years of fighting.

Therefore what happened once and for all is not passed. Jesus Christ, crucified under Pontius Pilate in the year 30, is no mere historical personality. If he were that, he would not be the Saviour for all times. Instead he is the living present Christ, our Lord, who dwells in us by his word and our faith, who is the living Head of the living body of the Church. At this point the parable of D-day collapses. D-day is passed even if its effects go on. But Jesus Christ is not merely present in his effects but personally, yesterday, today and in eternity the same. Just as the sap of the vine circulates in the branches, makes them living and holds them together, so is he, the Lord, present in his ecclesia, making it a unity, transforming it from day to day to make it more like him. But this is not enough; Jesus is also the future one. He is our future. The community of believers, as the New Testament depicts it, is a society of men who are watching intently for something which is to come. They call this, which is to come, the day of Jesus Christ. The same apostle, who in the words quoted has directed our glance backward to the event on the cross, can say of himself in his letter to the Philippians, 'Forgetting the things which are behind, stretching forward to the things which are before, I press on towards the goal unto the prize of the high calling of God in Christ Jesus.' It is the picture of a runner on the race-course—a picture which is very often used in the New Testament—who fixes his eyes on the goal, concentrates every thought upon it and puts in the last reserves of his energy to reach it. So the followers of Christ are intent upon the goal towards which they are running.

Here, finally, seems to be the point where our optimistic view of the future and the New Testament message meet. Is it not that idea of a better future which moves us? Is it not that idea which gives power to our activity, which makes us endure sacrifice and give ourselves? Is it not this idea of the coming kingdom of God, which, unlike any other idea of the Bible, fills us with joy and with the feeling that our life has a meaning and is worth living? What oxygen is for the lungs and the blood, hope is for the soul. After all, that is the ultimate meaning of the Christian faith.

We have to be careful, however, that we may not in the end fall victims to a fatal illusion. After we have seen how different from our way of thinking is the relation of the New Testament to the time-process, what a paradoxical role the idea of onceness plays within it and how this historical onceness is at the same time present, we may expect that the New Testament idea of the future is also very different from ours. If we think of the future, we see before us a series of successive intermediate goals, each successive one being nearer the final goal. We therefore think that we are approaching step by step to the condition which we think is the final one. We think of a goal to be realized more and more in the course of time.

Whether you use the word progress for this, or for certain reasons do not use it, whether you think these intermediate goals more continuously linked with each other, or whether your idea is more that of a dramatic series of pushes, in all cases the common element is this, that later generations will be nearer the goal, that their conditions of life, their social institutions, their political and cultural conditions will be more similar to the final end than ours. This is a picture of the future which is closely related to our own doing. If the craftsman works upon a piece of wood or leather, he thinks of what shall come out of it, and sees to it that by his work the unshaped raw material becomes the object which he had in mind. The same is true of the work of an artist, of an educator, of a social worker or social reformer and of a statesman. Wherever meaningful work is done, there is a process by which raw material, something which is not as it ought to be, becomes, by methodical work, more and more what it ought to be. Every worker has in his mind a plan or sketch of the final outcome and this plan directs every phase of his actions. Otherwise his action could not be meaningful.

Now there is no doubt that this kind of realization by an action towards something better, is given its place in the biblical message as well; wherever men's doings are spoken of and wherever something is expected from their doing, we find this familiar picture of meaningful work according to the rules of craftsmanship. Or we find a similar picture in natural life, the picture of natural growth. In the life of a Christian also there should be a growth, a progress, an enlargement, an enrichment. There should be a spreading of the Christian community. But this is only one side of the picture; alongside these ideas of growth and progress are those in which the life of the believers is represented in the opposite way. With a curious insistence the New Testament speaks of a gradual dying of man, of a building as it were not upwards, but downwards. In the centre of the New Testament, where the cross of Christ stands, this downward movement is concentrated. It is in connexion with the cross that this negative sight of man's work is presented. It is not man's work which matters, but God's; it is not by works that salvation comes, but by faith, not by action, but by passion. Again we meet the same paradox, the same connexion of elements which are contradictory and irreconcilable for our thinking. On the one hand the Christian is to use all his energy as if salvation were dependent upon his own exertion and on the other hand it is said that God alone brings about salvation and man's doing is vain. On the one hand the highest moral demands are made upon man's will, higher than anywhere else, and on the other hand all moral effort is completely devaluated, and confidence in those efforts is said to be the greatest hindrance to Christian faith.

We have come to grips with this problem because natural thinking, and particularly the thinking of modern man, sees the realization of the divine world-purpose, the coming of the kingdom of God, on analogy with meaningful human action as represented in the example of craftsmanlike procedure. Now we look again at the biblical idea of the future. Indeed it is the divine aim, the coming of the kingdom, the perfection of all things, upon which the heart and mind of the New Testament community are directed. It is from this expectation that the Christian's life receives its incomparable tension and power. But now we see that this aim and the manner of its realization are fundamentally different from our rational idea of future aims and therefore totally different from the modern interpretation of the kingdom of God and its coming. Once more let us hear the apostle Paul. Only a few lines after those words which we quoted about forgetting that which lies behind and stretching out to that which is before him, he says: 'For our citizenship is in heaven; from whence also we wait for a Saviour, the Lord Jesus Christ; who shall fashion anew the body of our humiliation, that it may be conformed to the body of his glory, according to the working whereby he is able even to subject all things unto himself.'

Now this picture is just the reverse of ours. This is not a movement going on from where we are, step by step, until the goal is reached, not a movement going upwards, as it were on a ladder until the highest point is reached, the movement of Dante from hell through purgatory to heaven; but on the contrary, it is a movement starting from heaven, starting from where God is, and going downwards to us until we are reached. It is, as we can easily see, the same movement of which we heard in the previous lecture, namely the movement of the Son of God taking the form of a servant, becoming obedient unto the death on the cross. Only this time the final point of this movement is no more the death on the cross, but our resurrection, the transformation of our body of humility into Christ's body of glory. And just as the first movement, ending on the cross, had the character of a oneness, so too has the second. As there was a D-day on which the dark powers were broken on the cross, so there will be a V-day on which the victory, until then hidden, breaks into visibility, a real victory-day. The New Testament calls this day emphatically the day of the Lord Jesus Christ. This then is the goal towards which the Christian life is directed and its race run. From there we understand the otherwise paradoxical character of man's movement of which we were just speaking. Because it is a participation both in the cross of Christ, in his dying, in his humiliation, and at the same time in his resurrection and his coming in power, because both these days are, so to speak, foreshadowed in Christian life—that is why it is so contradictory.

All three dimensions of time, the past, the present and the future, form a paradoxical unity in the Christian existence. And it is just this paradoxical unity which is the power of God working in man and in the history of mankind towards the aim of perfection and salvation. The Christian is one with Christ crucified by faith; he is one with the Christ present by participating in his love and communion. The Christian is expecting the victory day of resurrection, having part in it already now and here, by living hope; and this hope is not only the great joy and comfort but also the great moving power of his life and action. But this hope cannot stand by itself; it is what it must be only in its unity with faith and love. This is the three-dimensional existence in time of the Christian Church.

But finally it is this knowledge of the end, the *telos*, which gives the Christian life its meaning, and thereby its power. This then is the Christian dynamism. The content of this happening is most fully and best rendered by the word 'resurrection.' The day of Jesus Christ is the day of resurrection, that is to say, it is an event which cannot take place gradually and which leaves no room for realization in steps. Between the life of man in his mortal body and the resurrection, there are no transitions, there is no approximation between the two, there is a clear sharp line of demarcation. And this is exactly the sharp contrast to our natural thinking of the future aim, for which the idea of approximation is characteristic. You cannot be more or less reawakened in the life of resurrection. Either you live, as we all do, in this body, which is a body of death, or you are living in a new kind of existence which does not know death. All continuity from one to the other, by successive states of realization, is excluded. Second, this event is one which comes exclusively from God's side and not from ours. With the powers given him by God man can do many things, but one thing he cannot do, free himself from death and transform his body into the body of glory and eternal life. Even the Christian, who certainly can do many things which no other can, if he is really filled with love, springing from faith—even he cannot do that. It is true, there is a transformation of the character of our life, which, as the apostle says, makes us more similar to Christ from day to day. But this transformation remains even at its best within the limits of the mortal body, of the body of flesh. It is true that the life of the Christian is meant to become more and more similar to the image of Jesus, and to deny this would mean to deny the power of the Holy Spirit. But with all that included, all this transformation, even to its highest degree, is merely a transformation within the limits of this world of mortality. It is a life by faith and not by sight.

Why is it that the Bible places such emphasis on this line of demarcation between the body of death and the body of resurrection? Would it not be justifiable to think that the main thing is that inner change, which is possible already in this historical time and the present form of existence, so that resurrection would be simply the final crowning event, the last and short fragment of the long way previously traversed? The New Testament does not allow such an interruption. The body of death is not a mere detail, a mere detail of a negative character, which in the end will be taken care of. The body of death is a terrific totalitarian reality which forms the character of this our existence, the contradictory character of historical life. Once more our moral pride is seriously cast down. In spite of all changes or transformations, be they in the life of individuals or in the life of social institutions, of states and nations, one thing remains unchanged, and that is the contradictory character, the problematic, uncertain, fragile, mixed character of this sinful existence, which everywhere shows the sign of death.

The body of death does not mean simply that we die physically, although this in itself is a fact of overwhelming importance. It is no small thing, that all of us have to die and that neither all our progress in science, medicine and technology, nor any transformation by moral and religious forces, even those which true faith produces, can in any way alter that fact. But this is not the whole truth. In the New Testament, death and the body of death mean something much larger. The body of death is the historical, earthly existence as such, which in its deepest roots is affected by the separation from God and is for that reason self-contradictory in its whole character. Even the Christians, the best, the most faithful, the most loving members of the body of Christ, are living within or together with this body of death until the day of resurrection. That means that they, like the rest of men, become sick and weak, that in them, as in the others, there is a fear of death never completely to be overcome; whoever denies that, is living in a great self-illusion. Moreover, to live in the body of death means that Christians also carry their heavenly treasure in earthly vessels, that even in them all that comes from Christ is darkened again and again by what comes out of sin, so that even in them, above all in them, there is an unceasing battle going on between that which is from above and that which is from below, that even they, the saints of God, are sinners, although their sin is dead in so far as they are living in Christ.

One more thing has to be said about the body of death: it is the indissoluble connexion with the world, which is estranged from God and contradicts the gospel of Jesus Christ. It is at this point that the contrast between the New Testament hope and the idea of progress manifests itself most clearly. Nowhere in the New Testament do we find any expectation that in the course of the centuries mankind will become Christian, so that the opposition between the world and the Church would be overcome in historical time. But the contrary is true: the Christian community or Church will be a minority until the end, and therefore the battle between the dark powers and the powers of Christ goes on until the day of judgment. If there is any truth in the apocalyptic pictures which we find in the New Testament, we have to say even more. The apocalyptic visions are unanimous in depicting the end of time, the last phase of human history before the coming of the day of Christ, as a time of uttermost tension between light and darkness, the Church and the world, Christ and the Devil. Certainly the Church of Christ is moving on, is spreading over the surface of the earth. It may be that it is growing inwardly in power and outwardly in extent and influence, but at the same time the powers of evil are growing too and are capable of using the progress made by mankind in bringing natural forces into its service. In other words, the picture which the New Testament gives of the historical process until the day of Christ is in exact concordance with historical reality as we know it, and therefore in strictest opposition to the modern idea of progress, even in its pseudo-Christian form which mistakenly sees the New Testament gospel of the coming kingdom as an immanent upward movement. Nowhere does the New Testament promise an earthly state of peace, of social justice, or universal international relationships conforming to the idea of justice and humanity.

Why not? Because the body of death is a terrific reality. It is that, even for Christians who are faithful followers of their Lord. It is much more so in the world, which is not subdued to Christ. I think it is justifiable to interpret the idea of the anti-Christ in such a way that it means the growing tension between the forces of God, given to his Church, and the forces of evil, progressing in the world. In the measure that the Spirit of Christ manifests himself powerfully within the Church, in that measure the world reacts so much more passionately against him. The better the Church, the greater the exertions of the diabolic forces to keep their own. Judged by this picture of temporal history every conception of the time-process influenced by the idea of progress is unmasked as utopian, contradicted by reality just as much as by biblical doctrine.

All this, however, is only the negative side of the great positive message about the goal of human life and of the world at large. Utopianism is not too great, but too small a hope, since it is limited by the historical horizon. The hope we have in Jesus Christ goes beyond history. History cannot contain what God has in store for us. Historical life is temporal life; historical changes are temporal changes and historical gains and losses are temporal gains and losses. The perspective of the gospel is eternity. Anything perfect cannot be brought about in the narrow frame of temporality and terrestrial life. The perfection and fulfilment for which God has created us are of such a nature that they break this narrow frame. God's love goes beyond history, of which death is so characteristic a feature. Resurrection is eternal life breaking up the framework of historical existence. God, who has come down to us in the form of man in order to share with us his own life, wants us to take part in his eternal love and life. It is not for a certain space of time only that he wants to have communion with us. As his love is unconditional with regard to sin, so it is unconditional with regard to death. Whatever may be the course of history, the end of history shall be beyond history and this end is the perfection of God's creation and the realization of God's reign of holiness and love in eternal life.

That is why utopias of historical progress cannot seduce those who believe in Christ. Utopias are the straws to which those cling who have no real hope; utopias are as unattractive as they are incredible for those who know what real hope is. Utopias are not a consequence of true hope but a poor substitute for it and therefore a hindrance and not a help. The hope that is in Jesus Christ is different from all utopias of universal progress. It is based on the revelation of God's plan in the revelation of the crucified one. It is, therefore, not an uncertain speculation about the future but a certainty based upon what God has already revealed. One cannot believe in Jesus Christ without knowing for certain that God's victory over all powers of destruction, including death, is the end towards which the time-process moves as its own end.

We have come to the close of our lectures. Historical revelation, the triune God, original sin, Christ the Mediator, resurrection—these are some of the main doctrines of Christianity and, at the same time, some of the main stumbling-blocks which this gospel presents to modern thinking. If we penetrate deeply enough into each one of these topics we shall see that they are not so much different doctrines but different aspects of one and the same truth. The Christian doctrine does not consist of parts but is of one piece. It is one of the tasks of systematic theology to make this clear, to show the coherence of what we at first sight might call different doctrines. It is by historical revelation that we know of the triune God, of original sin, of the reconciling work of Christ and of the consummation of the world in eternal life. It is because of our sin that we need reconciliation. It is the triune God who reveals himself and reconciles us to himself in Jesus Christ. Each one of these doctrines points to the other as its complement, each one of them cannot be properly understood without the others. Each one of these doctrines is essential for and characteristic of the Christian faith. None of the non-Christian religions, none of the philosophical systems of theology, has any of these doctrines. They are absolutely specifically doctrines belonging to the Christian gospel, and whatever similarities in non-Christian theology might be pointed to are but faint and uncertain analogies.

Moreover, as we have tried to show, the acceptance of each of these doctrines is not a matter of authoritarian belief but a matter of existential or ethical decision. They all lead to a point where man has to give account of his own existence, his moral condition, his self-evaluation, his understanding of himself. Each one of them points towards that narrow gate through which alone he can enter into real communion with God and into eternal life. Whether one believes in these doctrines is therefore not a matter of mere belief, but a matter of life decision. They are not merely a matter of religious opinion which you may or may not have, but of a different condition and character of life which distinguishes the one who does and the one who does not believe in them.

Therefore they are all, from the point of view of natural thinking, of man's own wisdom, the same foolishness, one and the same scandal of Christianity. It is one of the greatest dangers of the Church in a democratic country—and one of the greatest temptations for churches which for their support are dependent on the good will of their congregations—to present the gospel message in a way agreeable and inoffensive to those who are to hear it. As most of the public who attend cinema shows demand that the show should have a happy end, so most of the churchgoers desire to get a message which is pleasing to hear. Now in the last analysis the gospel *is* pleasing to hear, otherwise it would not be called the good tidings. But it is pleasing to hear only for those who are poor in their hearts, thirsty and self-despairing, it is certainly not pleasing to any kind of happy-end mentality. It is not pleasing but shocking to all those who want to be confirmed in their natural inclinations of thinking and willing, in their modernist outlook, in their rational self-affirmation. Through the whole Bible runs that conception that God is near to broken hearts only and not to proud and self-sufficient minds. The Gospel is that kind of religious truth which makes man utterly dependent on God and utterly un-self-sufficient, whilst idealism or mystical religion is, in the last analysis, flattering to man and therefore pleasant to hear. That is why the gospel will and must be unpopular—in fact the very opposite of popular—and wherever the Church becomes very popular the suspicion cannot be far away that such a church is catering to the public by falsifying the gospel. To live by that truth which is foolishness to the wise and a stumbling-block to the moralists, is certainly not a popular thing. But this is the touchstone of the gospel. Where it is not foolishness and scandalous in the sense of the apostles, it certainly is not the gospel, but some kind of idealism disguised in gospel terminology.

On the other hand it must also be said that not every kind of foolishness or scandal is that of the gospel. The Christian scandal is that alone which is foolish to the wise and scandalous to the moral people, in that it contains God's wisdom and righteousness. The Church has failed not only by dodging the offence which the gospel offers, but also by wrapping the gospel in language and concepts which are mere human primitiveness and superstition. Do not let us forget that all the treasures of wisdom are hid in Christ. The Christian message is not opposed to hard and deep thinking, granted that this thinking is done to honour God's wisdom and not man's. At the present time, when man is filled with his own wisdom, the gospel truth will hardly seize man's heart without forcing upon him some hard thinking. The gospel does not encourage thoughtlessness, just as little as it encourages moral sloth. It is by taking seriously the task of thinking as well as the task of being good, that it breaks through rationalism and through moralism. It is by fulfilling the law that Christ has made us free from the curse of the law, but made us free in such a way that we are so much the more bound by God himself.

Let me say one last word. The scandal of Christianity exists as a scandal only so long as we are full of ourselves. To believe in the cross of Christ is no scandal for those who have seen how perverted is their own wisdom, the wisdom of natural man. It is the very corrective for this perversion of our sight, it makes us look straight again, who by sin have become cross-eyed. The foolishness of the gospel is divine wisdom to all those who have been healed of the perversion which consists in making man's reason and goodness the judge of all truth, that perversion which places man instead of God in the centre of the universe. The gospel is identical with the healing of this perversion, which in its depth and real significance is diabolical. It is the victory of God's light over the powers of darkness.